Praise for *Beyond Discomfort*

One of the few books I have read on diversity, inclusion and equality which made me stop and reflect on what it takes to be a truly inclusive leader. Beyond Discomfort challenged some of my own belief systems or 'Way of Being', held sincerely and in good faith, with thought-provoking, real-life examples viewed through a different lens. I would recommend this book to any leader who is serious about DEI and initiating real change in both their own mindsets and the culture of their business.

Ben Allen
Chief Executive Officer, Mark Allen Group

Nadia's approach to the subject of inclusion is incredibly thought-provoking, challenging us to notice how our learned values and beliefs can inform how we live and lead. The 'Way of Being' provides an accessible and, importantly, non-judgemental continuum with which to recognize where we and others may be on this journey. I highly recommend Beyond Discomfort, not only for leaders in business and the People profession, but for anyone who is curious and seeking to understand how to engender greater inclusion.

Greg Bloomer
People Director, Centrica

Nadia welcomes leaders to not just acknowledge the discomfort and complexity that always come with change, but equips readers with her innovative model and numerous compelling examples that help guide leaders through that complexity to the transformation ahead. She is that rare voice that makes space for learners at all points in their journey. This is an exciting contribution to building a more inclusive future!

Jennifer Brown
Keynoter & WSJ best-selling author of How to Be an Inclusive Leader

A pragmatic, realistic approach that puts leaders at the centre of their journey to inclusion. Nadia uses her knowledge of psychology to unpick the way we work, lead and interact with each other. She doesn't shy away from uncomfortable scenarios and questions – questions we may have had ourselves, or heard from others. I have been able to successfully apply her practical framework and question guides to some tricky corporate problems and conversations.

Camilla Bruggen
Global Head of Diversity, Equity and Inclusion, Wavemaker

A very candid, conversational read that touches upon so many critical topics that we must discuss and embrace as leaders. Beyond Discomfort invites us to lean into transparent conversations, bring diversity to the table and open our minds to an ever-evolving world.

Michelle Chin
Vice President, Starbucks EMEA

Wow, Beyond Discomfort is fabulous! For me, what stands this apart from the numerous other DEI books is how Nadia has woven so many lived experiences into the narrative. She sensitively guides us to reflect on our own perspectives in a way that challenges our thinking and creates space for inclusive practices. I would highly recommend all DEI enablers and leaders read this book.

Chrissie Clarke
Vice President, Diversity, Inclusion and Engagement, Wood

Vital reading for those wanting to navigate inclusion from a deeper perspective. Nadia surfaces the difficulties of our implicit errors of thinking and has captured these in four stances, which we might variously occupy. With numerous relevant examples, she shows us how these stances manifest and how we can overcome them.

Claire Collins
Emerita Professor of Leadership, Henley Business School, University of Reading

Practical, insightful, challenging and a call to action for all. Beyond Discomfort shares how, through a clear and simple description of four Ways of Being, change is possible. For leaders, for DEI professionals and for those who want to move from bystander to upstander.

Genevieve Glover
Chair, RFU Inclusion & Diversity & RFU Council Member
Chief People Officer, Barchester Healthcare

Wanting to be inclusive, and thinking we are, isn't enough — we must change the way we act and make decisions. Beyond Discomfort gives you real-life examples, ideas and the impetus to be an inclusive leader who can make a real difference at work and in the world.

Gethin Nadin
Best-selling HR author & HR Most Influential Thinker 2023
Chief Innovation Officer, Benefex

Simply put, this book is an excellent read. Nadia uses everyday examples to bring theory to life. The non-judgemental delivery of the observations is clever. As you journey through the pages, you build a level of confidence to self-reflect, explore and challenge your in-built, learnt belief systems. But to get the most out of this read, you need to be ready to fully open up and face into the areas you usually shy away from confronting.

Shelly Nash
People and Culture Director, London Marathon Group

Getting leaders to champion inclusion across their work can often be challenging. Nadia's book insightfully summarizes the multiple reasons why this is the case. It sets out the steps that every leader can take to make their organization truly inclusive whilst navigating the fear that inevitably accompanies this work.

Dr Asif Sadiq MBE
Chief Diversity, Equity and Inclusion Officer, Warner Bros. Discovery

An incisive, honest and, at times, confronting approach to one of the most relevant topics of our time. Beyond Discomfort provides a straightforward model for leaders to actually 'feel' the lens through which they approach DEI and offers practical steps for their own growth — and, consequently, the growth of those they lead — towards greater inclusion.

Rick Willis
President & CEO, Brain Injury Association of America

Beyond Discomfort

Why inclusive leadership is so hard

(and what you can do about it)

Nadia Nagamootoo

First published in Great Britain by Practical Inspiration Publishing, 2024

© Nadia Nagamootoo, 2024

The moral rights of the author have been asserted

ISBN   9781788604390 (PB)
        9781788605793 (HB)
        9781788604413 (epub)
        9781788604406 (mobi)

Every effort has been made to trace copyright holders and to obtain their permission for the use of copyright material. The publisher apologizes for any errors or omissions and would be grateful if notified of any corrections that should be incorporated in future reprints or editions of this book.

Want to bulk-buy copies of this book for your team and colleagues? We can customize the content and co-brand *Beyond Discomfort* to suit your business's needs.

Please email info@practicalinspiration.com for more details.

Practical Inspiration Publishing

For Ilana and Esmé, who are my reason why and ignite an even deeper passion for this work. Always remember — yes, it is possible and, yes, you can.

For Matthew, whose response to me whenever I explain my next ambitious goal can be summarized in four words — 'What do you need?' Thank you for your partnership, for continuously lifting me up and being my biggest advocate.

Contents

Foreword

Over the past few decades, the demands on organizations related to diversity, equity and inclusion (DEI) have not only expanded significantly but also increased in complexity. As a Black American woman and amputee, believe me, I understand! We've gone from talking about diversity and equal opportunity for all to realizing that the issues are much more systemic, deeply embedded in our history, politics and culture, and that the work towards inclusion was far more than we ever anticipated.

I have been on this journey with corporations, diversity professionals and individuals for decades now… and it has not gotten simpler or easier. Emotions have run high as the discourse has grown. People from marginalized groups finally feel like they have been given a platform to share their experiences, and naturally there is a lot of pain, hurt and anger there. The number of DEI practitioners entering the field and supporting the cause has grown substantially, with lots of passion and good intentions of leveraging their own lived experiences to generate change. However, it is an eclectic group, some of whom haven't trained in the areas of systemic transformation or understanding human behaviour. As a result, we have fallen into a common human pitfall whereby DEI is now seen as 'fighting the good fight' to claim back from the majority what has, over the centuries, been denied or taken away from marginalized communities.

However, as we attempt to rebalance the inequity, fight injustice and push for organizations to do more to embrace DEI, those in majority groups are experiencing emotions that are akin to being wrongly accused of a crime. Sadly, the inevitable consequence is an enhanced feeling of 'us versus them'. This is, of course, the opposite of what we want to achieve. We see the consequences of this pushback to DEI in the media, political news and organizational leadership decisions; sometimes it feels like progress is not only stalling but in reverse.

As such, this book, which injects an invaluable perspective on today's DEI challenges, couldn't be more timely. We urgently need to reframe DEI, its purpose and how we achieve it. The Beyond Discomfort® model is a highly accessible way of explaining the current state of play in DEI from an emotions- and values-based perspective. This is crucial for real change. It's not enough to simply explain to leaders what they need to do – this won't make a difference if DEI fundamentally jars with their world view. We need all leaders to actively engage in DEI for the inclusion of all. We need to *feel* it as well as think it.

Nadia offers her wealth of knowledge as a guide for all of us – those who are experienced in the field as well as newcomers – to engage and do our best work. Her engaging writing style, candour and insight into creating real impact combine to offer an entertaining journey that is both practical and wise. What we need is for *all* leaders, no matter their background or world view, to read this book. It provides the tools to develop your ability to self-reflect, understand your values and emotional triggers when it comes to DEI and be able to navigate Beyond Discomfort. So, read the book, do the work and spread the word far and wide.

Bonnie St. John
CEO, Blue Circle Leadership
Paralympic medalist, best-selling author and international speaker

Introduction

When my husband and I decided to get married, we had a long discussion about what our surname was going to be. My family name is Nagamootoo and his family name is Smith.

I am first-generation UK-born with a Mauritian heritage. I am proud of this heritage as much as I am proud to be British. Not only does my surname signal this important part of my identity, but I am also fortunate that it is pretty unique and therefore memorable. As a bonus, I have a decent number of 'a's and 'o's in my surname, which often made me a winner in the playground when we played Red Letter (a game where having a long name and multiples of the same letter counted for a lot).

I didn't have anything against being a Smith, but even in my late twenties I knew I wanted the type of career that would have a public profile, and so using any leverage I could get to stand out from the crowd would be helpful.

It's also worth bearing in mind that by then I already had plenty of experience of being overlooked and underestimated due to my petite stature, ethnic background and hereditary youthful looks (for which I am most thankful now I am in my forties!). I learnt to compensate for these hurdles of physicality by ensuring I was one of the first to speak when meeting new people, reeling off my credentials by way of introduction and injecting confidence in my voice.

Anyway, back to the surname debate. As you can imagine, this wasn't the type of quick, easily solved conversation you might have to, say, decide what colour to paint the living room. This was the type of complex, meaty and not so clear-cut conversation that pops up every so often, generates a few options but never reaches a conclusion. So, the conversations continued, and we got family members and friends involved as we toyed with variants. I could be Nagamootoo professionally and change my name to Smith for everything else… rejected for being a bit complicated. I could be Nagamootoo and my husband and any future kids could be Smith… rejected in favour of us all sharing the same family name. We could mesh our names and be Nagamith or Smootoo… rejected, no explanation needed! This went on until there was only one remaining logical decision – he would change his name to Nagamootoo.

There were already two other people with the same surname as him in his relatively small company, so it quite appealed to him to have a more unique name. And he also appreciated that since any children we had would be born and brought up in the British culture, carrying a Mauritian surname would offer them an anchor to their heritage. For him, going against tradition and changing his name to mine wasn't a big deal. What's in a name, right? Well, it turns out there's a lot in a name which we hadn't fully accounted for.

When I told one of my friends, she stared at me in surprise and asked: 'How do his parents feel about him leaving the family?'

'What do you mean "leaving the family"? He's no less part of their family just because his name is changing', I replied in both shock and annoyance at her belligerent attitude.

And here lies the fundamental flaw in our analysis. We had forgotten to take into consideration the significance of history, tradition and societal values. Think of all the gender-based symbols and expectations involved in marriage – the man proposing, the father giving away the bride, the bride leaving her family to be provided for by her husband whilst she cares for him and the children. The concept of marriage is steeped in patriarchy, power and inequity.

When my husband told his work colleagues that he was changing his name to mine, a few of them made remarks like '*I can see who wears the trousers in your relationship.*'

To us, our marriage was two people coming together as equals and joining each other's families in equal measure. Our choice of surname had no bearing on our perspective of each other's families or on how we acted or behaved within each family. To the Western world, our choice of surname indicated a role reversal. The perception was that I now had more power and he was less of a man (in the traditional sense of being the provider for our family). My family was more dominant, and I had rejected entering his.

I share this story with you for two reasons. Firstly, it is a reminder of the importance of history, culture and values in decision-making. This doesn't mean that we would have altered anything about our choice of family name, but simply that it would have helped us better deliver the news and manage the expectations of our families if we had considered the wider perspective. Secondly, it is a reminder that challenging inequity and disrupting the status quo will inevitably lead to upset. Why? Because this is deeply uncomfortable and eats away at the core of who we are.

The act of my husband changing his surname to mine challenged the patriarchy and inequity of marriage. We hadn't appreciated how much we were asking of our families – that they let go of this traditional concept and move 'Beyond Discomfort' to accept that our choice was actually a rebalancing of our roles in marriage that brought down the power structures embedded in the system and created a beautiful parity between two families. It was a lot to ask without an explanation, or a guiding hand anyway.

In a similar way, we can't simply expect leaders to immediately embrace diversity, equity and inclusion (DEI) when it doesn't necessarily make sense to them or fit with their established ways of seeing the world. Leading inclusively is tough because you have to constantly challenge yourself to operate Beyond Discomfort. This means fighting back the urge to remain fixed in your mindset and hold on to an entrenched view of how right you are. It means being able to reflect and analyse where your beliefs, values and rules about life come from (historically, socially and culturally) and to accept that there are multiple perspectives and that what is 'right' may not always be clear. It means looking for and noticing the hidden and intangible inequities deep within our organizational structures and searching for a way forward that offers justice and fairness, even though outwardly it may look like sacrificing the power of those who currently have it. It means acknowledging that an imperfect system elevates some at the cost of others and that a redistribution of power will have consequences for all. And it means being continuously cognizant of your own emotions and the fears that inevitably arise when there is change and uncertainty, and pushing yourself to have brave new conversations that educate and expand your understanding of those who are different to you.

Having started to unpack, through my personal story, why DEI is both challenging and uncomfortable, let me offer you a broader understanding of what sits at the core of who we are and how we see the world.

An ontological approach to diversity, equity and inclusion

Several years ago, I qualified as an ontological coach. In essence, this approach focuses on a person's 'Way of Being', or how they interact with the world based on the set of values and beliefs they have accumulated throughout their life. In *Coaching to the Human Soul*, Alan Sieler, Founder and Director of the Ontological Coaching Institute, describes Way of Being as 'How we are at any point in time, and in particular... how we are observing and perceiving the world.'[1]

As an example, when my mum was growing up in Mauritius, there were often wild dogs roaming the streets, and she was taught by her parents that they were dangerous and to steer clear. This instilled a belief in her that all dogs are dangerous, and so, as a little girl, I would often feel her anxiety and her hand tightening around mine whenever we walked past a dog in the street. Unsurprisingly, I too learnt that all dogs are dangerous, and even now, despite knowing logically that this isn't true, I still feel a sense of unease when a dog is present.

My mum's Way of Being – her narrative about dogs, the emotions she experienced around them and what she felt in her body – led to various behaviours, such as crossing the street if a dog was coming towards her or avoiding going to a friend's house if they owned a dog. And an unintended outcome of this was that I observed her Way of Being and absorbed it as my own.

As Sieler explains: 'We do not see how things are; we see them according to how we are.' This is such a powerful statement and helps us understand why inclusive leadership is so hard. It challenges us at the deepest level of who we are and requires us to shift aspects of our Way of Being – that is, how we have observed the world and what we therefore know to be true. As soon as we allow space for someone else's narrative and open ourselves to the possibility of seeing things differently, it naturally changes how we participate in the world.

Let's take the simple example of a man opening a door for a woman, or the concept of 'ladies first'. This White, European tradition dates back to medieval times when knights showed courtesy and respect to women by helping them through doors as they needed both hands to lift their heavy dresses off the floor in order to walk. This value of chivalry has stood the test of time with the belief that it's gentlemanly to hold the door open for a woman. However, the underlying narrative here which is potentially harmful to equity and inclusion is that men are stronger and women need to be cared for by them.

Notice in yourself any visceral reaction to reading this. What emotion does it provoke in you? Common male responses are: '*That's absolutely* ridiculous. Now men can't even hold a door open for a woman without being called sexist – we can't win'; or 'Surely opening a door for a woman or letting her go first is just being polite – how can that be sexist?'

For those readers who are men, if you noticed any defensiveness within you, it's probably because a core part of who you are – your Way of Being – has been bruised by what seems like an accusation of sexist behaviour rather than a recognition of an act of kindness.

Let's look at this from a different angle. On International Women's Day in 2015, Emma Watson, actor and Goodwill Ambassador for UN Women, landed a powerful point during a Q&A at Facebook's London headquarters: 'I love having the door opened for me and I love being taken out to dinner; it's so great. I think the key is would you then mind if I opened the door for you?'[2]

Her point is that the concept of chivalry is gendered, but it doesn't have to be. Women can be chivalrous too – after all, it is just about being polite and kind to one another. Even so, in order for a man to accept a woman's offer to pay for the meal on their first date, he has to shift his Way of Being, recognize the emotional discomfort he feels, the thought that 'this isn't the way it should be', and move beyond that. In this case, moving Beyond Discomfort requires him to reassess his deeply held beliefs that the man should pay and provide for the woman, recognizing it comes from a time when women were financially dependent and needed this level of support. He probably also needs to get over the lurking inner voice that's asking 'What will people say if they found out she paid?!', reflecting the natural fear that surfaces when we go against the status quo. And he needs to be able to embrace a new perspective which views this new relationship as two people coming together as equals. That's a lot to process, especially if he has to do it in the moment, but the outcome of all this deep inner work would be that he smiles, accepts her act of kindness and thanks her for a lovely dinner.

I will talk more about the concepts of equality and equity in Chapter 4, but first let me explain more about this book and what you can expect.

A new lens on inclusive leadership

An inclusive leader has to be skilful, adept and well practised in self-reflection. They must understand their Way of Being – where their beliefs come from – and be able to respond within seconds in a way that embraces a view different from their own. That's no mean feat.

I've written Beyond Discomfort because I witness the struggle that people face with embodying inclusion in daily life – not just clients and colleagues (working in the space of DEI automatically opens up conversations you wouldn't typically have) but also friends and family. I am privileged to have connected with and shared learning spaces with thousands of leaders globally to help them unravel the knotty, complex tensions that DEI brings.

In my work with clients, I have often been called upon to run inclusive leadership programmes. It starts with a module that gets to the heart of why leaders need to look inwards at their own Way of Being, their own beliefs and biases, as well as to where power and inequity plays out in organizational life. By the end of this first session, I am never surprised, though I always experience a pang of disappointment, when one or two of the evaluation responses say things like: 'Great session but I'm left not knowing what I'm meant to do with this. Would be helpful to have more tips and advice on how to be inclusive.' These leaders want a quick fix, along the lines of: 'Tell me what to do, I'll do it and then be on my way.' This may also indicate the value their organizations place on learning.

But in order to be truly inclusive, leaders need to demonstrate a 'Receptiveness to Learn'. This is not just about learning what they need to do as an inclusive leader, but about educating themselves on history and cultures different from their own and delving deeply into learning about themselves. This includes an openness to learning by doing. I often come across leaders who are keen to be DEI allies but are paralysed for fear of overstepping and being accused of 'saviourism'. I'll discuss this further in Chapter 5.

They also need to show a 'Willingness to Act', not just passively – by liking other people's woke comments, for instance – but constantly dismantling the inequities around them and challenging themselves and their colleagues to promote inclusion at times when accepting the status quo would be far easier and more comfortable.

The Beyond Discomfort® model that I present in this book doesn't come from formal research. It comes from a lived place in the DEI field and insightful conversations on my podcast, Why Care?, interwoven with my professional experience as a chartered psychologist and accredited coach. When reflecting on my experience of working with leaders, I realized that these two concepts – Receptiveness to Learn and Willingness to Act – are related continuums, and I had met a variety of leaders operating at different points on them. These continuums make up the axes of the model.

For simplicity, I offer these to you in the form of four Ways of Being: Disconcerted, Proof-Seeking, Cheerleading and Beyond Discomfort. In reality, we know that humans are far more complex than this. But I hope that the stories and examples I share throughout the book, showing what leaders have told me they struggle with the most, will help facilitate your own thinking and help you unpick the complexity in your own head. Here are some of the narratives that I regularly come across with leaders who have gotten stuck – as you read them, reflect on whether you share that perspective or have similar questions:

o   DEI has overstepped the mark – it's now unfavourable to be a White, cisgender, heterosexual man.

o   If we positively discriminate in order to create equity, how will we know when we've got there and when to stop?

o   Are you saying: 'I've had it easy just because I'm White? I grew up in a low-income family and I've had my fair share of being bullied. I've earned my place.'

o   Surely by telling me that I need to see your difference is further creating an 'us versus them' situation? Shouldn't we just see everyone as equals and treat them all the same?

o   How are we meant to get diversity in the workplace when the issue is societal – there aren't enough people of diverse backgrounds choosing a career in our industry.

Notice that I have deliberately chosen the term Way of Being rather than words such as 'type' or 'trait'. Whereas, linguistically, leadership type or trait sounds more fixed and ingrained, a person's Way of Being, based on their experience and observations of the world, is malleable and can change with self-understanding, curiosity and open-mindedness. However, change is never easy. As established in the prominent work of Swiss American psychiatrist Elisabeth Kübler-Ross, change comes with inevitable waves of emotion: denial, anger, bargaining ('if only I had done it differently'), depression and acceptance.[3] Similarly, when working towards leadership Beyond Discomfort, you may discover truths that are shocking and feel angry that your good intentions are being attacked, regretful as you realize past errors, sad as you uncover colleagues' stories of deep trauma and pain, and overwhelmed at the scale of change required, but also accepting of your role as an ally. Part of the work is noticing when you become emotionally triggered and how you show ongoing personal commitment to work through these moments with the goal of inclusion always in your consciousness.

It's important to note that the four Ways of Being are not a leadership barometer; the model is not a reflection of how good or bad, or how right or wrong, a leader is. There are no value judgements here. The model illustrates how a leader's Way of Being impacts their Receptiveness to Learn and their Willingness to Act, which in turn influences their day-to-day inclusive practices.

Beyond Discomfort® model

PROOF-SEEKING

LEADERS:

- operate with curiosity for DEI and consider how they might adapt their leadership accordingly
- need to really understand what inclusive leadership looks like before they will shift from their default style
- feel agitated at the lack of clarity and complexity that inclusive leadership presents and, as a result, hold back from taking action

BEYOND DISCOMFORT

LEADERS:

- are proactive in their learning approach to DEI and seek to deepen their awareness of societal power structures
- remain open to noticing how the world interacts with those who are different to them
- lean in to new and uncomfortable conversations to aid their inclusive endeavours

DISCONCERTED

LEADERS:

- value the traditional principles of leadership – e.g. being assertive, taking action, having the answers
- believe in a meritocratic system where individuals are rewarded and achieve success based on talent
- believe DEI has gone too far, with minority individuals favoured to the detriment of majority individuals

CHEERLEADING

LEADERS:

- believe the most respectful and fair leadership approach is to disregard differences between individuals
- believe in equality and treating everyone the same
- think that they already lead inclusively and see very little more they need to do

RECEPTIVENESS TO LEARN HIGH / LOW

WILLINGNESS TO ACT LOW — HIGH

How to use this book

The aim of this book is not to suggest that you place yet another label on yourself. Let's face it, the world already does a good enough job of putting people in boxes and expecting them to act within set parameters. This isn't about figuring out which of the four Ways of Being you are. As you delve deeper into each chapter, you may find that elements of two, three or all four resonate with you. And that, in many ways, is to be expected. It might be, for example, that a Hispanic, cisgender, female leader has moved Beyond Discomfort by asking an LGBTQ+ team member about their lived experience in the organization. However, she may seek more proof and greater clarity about how these insights could shape her interactions. I choose this example deliberately to highlight that this book isn't just for White, straight, male leaders. Whilst they are certainly a demographic who would benefit from reading this book, I believe the deep inner work that this book provokes is important for us all.

The other thing this book is not doing is condemning people for not leading Beyond Discomfort. Yes, it is true that by practising Beyond Discomfort as a Way of Being, you will more likely demonstrate inclusive leadership. And, yes, it is true that if we are to build a more equitable future, we need more leaders embracing this Way of Being. However, that doesn't mean any other Way of Being is wrong. Indeed, it has no doubt served you well and underpinned your career success to date. However, as author, psychologist and economist Daniel Kahneman says: 'We can be blind to the obvious, and we are also blind to our blindness.'[4] In other words, we rarely inwardly inquire how our Way of Being limits us, but it is only by doing so that we can realize our true potential as an inclusive leader.

The Beyond Discomfort® model offers an accessible way of presenting different underlying values, beliefs and ways of observing the world, for you to digest and use in a manner that most benefits you. Ultimately, I hope that you will use the self-insights you gain from considering your leadership in relation to the model to break down barriers for underrepresented people, create a culture that reinforces inclusive behaviour and actively build teams with a greater sense of belonging.

In Chapter 1, I provide an overview of the reality of today's world, signposting the considerable urgency for DEI work in organizations. The business case has never been clearer, but sometimes it helps to have the facts laid out in front of us to support our drive for action. In chapters 2 to 5, I focus on the model. Each Way of Being is described in turn and brought to life with stories and anecdotes offering insight into the underlying fears and emotions that are typically present. At the end of each chapter, you'll find some questions for reflection to help you navigate those fears and expand your Way of Being — that is, how you observe the world. I believe the foundational work around this comes from simply reading the book and using it to deepen your self-understanding, challenge your thinking and develop empathy for others. Following that, of course, comes application of this learning and the inevitable development of your leadership practice.

In the final chapter, I consider what an organization that operates Beyond Discomfort looks and feels like. I felt it was important to highlight the systemic change in organizational culture when all leaders are actively inclusive. This may feel like a pipe dream but, whilst I am not denying that it takes a huge amount of work to get there and it doesn't happen overnight, there are a small number of organizations that are close to achieving this.

One thing I invite you to do as you read this book is to be aware of the emotions it evokes in you. Notice when you feel uneasy, annoyed or defensive. When you have these moments, explore them more deeply by asking yourself:

o   What is it about what you read that provoked this response?

o   What specific emotion are you feeling?

o   What questions is it making you ask yourself?

o   What questions don't you want to ask yourself?

o   What questions or challenges do you have for me, as the author?

o   What has sparked your curiosity?

That vital step of noticing and being curious is key to any shift towards inclusive practice that you will make. As technology executive and author Sheryl Sandberg says in *Lean In*: 'We cannot change what we are not aware of, and once we are aware, we cannot help but change.'[5]

To support your learning and discover more about your Way of Being, you can take an online questionnaire at the Beyond Discomfort website (www.beyond-discomfort.com). You'll also find a growing range of tools to support you as well as an online community for the latest DEI discussions.

If you do this work on yourself, you will inevitably find that you start to approach other people's behaviour with the same level of curiosity. My genuine hope and aspiration is that this book offers you a greater ability to interpret other people's comments and actions when they don't appear to aligned with your own beliefs or views.

 Practising discomfort

Whether you're a leader, a DEI practitioner or have arrived here via another path, it is likely you will be reading this book with a dual lens — seeking self-development as well as learning ways to have more impact in your organization or with your clients.

The ball of string icon appears throughout the book to signpost practical ideas, tools and exercises that support inclusive practices. These might be activities that will support your own learning or things you can do with colleagues or leaders in your organization. I hope that the guidance will help you better understand yourself and open up new conversations in your organization.

1 Guiding forces of inclusion

We are now faced with the fact that tomorrow is today. We are confronted with the fierce urgency of now. In this unfolding conundrum of life and history, there is such a thing as being too late. This is no time for apathy or complacency. This is a time for vigorous and positive action.

—Martin Luther King Jr[1]

We've come a long way since discussions of diversity were purely around equal opportunity for all. It seems almost naive now, looking back, that we thought that simply by creating legislative anti-discrimination acts, a change in how we treat minority groups would ensue. Firstly, because policies and laws don't offer the educational upskilling or attitudinal shift required for societal change. Secondly, because it assumes that those policing these rules are free of bias and willing to abide by the rules (I think we have more than enough examples of where this has proven not to be the case). Thirdly, because it doesn't take into consideration the complex and often invisible ways discrimination plays out. For many organizations, conversations around diversity have had a narrow focus on gender (men and women), disability and perhaps ethnicity. Gradually, over the years, we have bravely expanded our exploration to race, religion, culture, sexual orientation, caste, neurodiversity, mental health, age and gender through a non-binary lens, to name a few.

It has only really been within the last 10 years that work in this space has broadened beyond diversity to consider equity, inclusion and belonging. This has moved the conversation from looking at representation across diverse characteristics to assessing the bias deep within the foundations and structures of the systems we operate in (society, organizations, teams, etc.) and how we create fairness and justice so everyone feels valued and able to contribute their unique perspectives.

The language used in these conversations has evolved too. For example, 'intersectionality', a term coined by civil rights activist Kimberlé Crenshaw back in 1989,[2] has only recently come into common-use DEI vocabulary as we have begun to realize the importance of how different dimensions of diversity overlay each other and create a cumulative impact of discrimination and oppression for individuals. For example, a White, non-native English speaking, Eastern European, LGBTQ+ woman living in Canada will experience a layering of prejudices related to these different characteristics, which create multiple barriers in her life. If we see her only as a White woman, we will miss the intricacies that contribute to her lived experience. Another term, 'gaslighting', derived from the 1930s British play *Gas Light*, has risen in use to describe the manipulative tactics sometimes leveraged by those in power to undermine minority individuals' perception of reality. These are just two examples of many, creating an extraordinary vocabulary of new concepts. Whilst language helps us construct meaning, it also creates greater scope for more complex conversations, misinterpretation and misunderstanding. Furthermore, as injustices are given labels and therefore made real, people from marginalized and minority groups have felt more legitimacy to expect change.

As a consequence, the speed at which DEI has entered our daily lives is phenomenal and, for many, overwhelming. Organizations large and small in most places around the world are discussing how to create a more inclusive culture, whether generated by a desire to do the right thing, to lead the way in their industry and remain competitive, to access a broader talent pool, to better meet their changing customer needs or to improve their bottom line. Conversations are far from limited to the business world though. We're surrounded by DEI on TV and in movies, and in the news and on social media when well-known people have or haven't got it right. It's present in the educational curriculum and, without doubt, in playground and school gate politics. It's embedded in every relationship we have and explains why we find our parents frustrating and why our children feel the same about us.

With such a push for progress on DEI, it is perfectly valid to want to know why. The whole premise of this book is an invitation to you as leaders to dedicate time to reflective inner work and become more aware of the lenses through which you see the world. In this fast-paced modern life, where there is always too much to do, very few will be willing to take this step without at least one very compelling reason. In this chapter, I discuss some of the reasons, including the most pertinent challenges we face today, the tangible and intangible economic benefits of embracing DEI, the specific concerns of parents, the perspective of younger generations and the future of work. Depending on your inclination, these reasons may appeal more to your 'head' (logic and fact) than your 'heart' (emotions, values and beliefs) or vice versa, but probably always a bit of both. This chapter aims to help you tap into your why in order to support the deeper learning and self-reflection required in the rest of the book. If you don't think you need the facts and figures, jump right ahead to Chapter 2.

Current-day living

Whilst it might sound cliché, I believe this decade to be one of the most challenging and uncertain periods in recent history. That isn't to dismiss or minimize what it was like living through the world wars or various periods of serious economic downturn, or in countries where there have been devastating times of civil unrest. Our current-day living is like permanently sitting on a high-thrill rollercoaster, but not necessarily out of choice.

Let's start with the obvious – Covid-19. If anything is going to hit at the first level of Maslow's hierarchy of needs, it's a global pandemic. This was about safety and survival, which always brings out both the best and worst in human nature. In the US, gun stores had queues outside, signalling a desperate need for protection; and in the UK, there were empty supermarket shelves where pasta, rice and toilet rolls once sat. As a psychologist, I continue to be fascinated by the difference in cultural response to this high-threat situation! Adapting to the new way of life was brutal – many of us feared stepping outside our front doors and were worried about touching anything in the outside world, and we had no idea when it would be over. And as a parent, I learnt the hard way that I was not cut out to home-school my children. Whilst we hope lockdown life is behind us, the trauma of the pandemic will long remain, with many still suffering physical and mental health issues as a result.

During this time, some widely reported examples of the worst of human behaviour were the murders of Ahmaud Arbery, Breonna Taylor and George Floyd in February, March and May 2020, respectively. These led to a tipping point. Members of BIPOC (Black, Indigenous, People of Colour) communities from all around the world, who have lived with prejudice and discrimination all their lives (as did their ancestors before them), were clear that the time had come to take a stand. These events came at a time when we had already started to see statistical differences in Covid-19 death rates across socio-economic and racial backgrounds. For me, the Black Lives Matter movement was more than a fight for racial justice; it was a powerful catalyst for bolder conversations and renewed energy to create equality for all minority groups. Where organizational DEI efforts had predominantly focused on issues of gender in a male/female binary way, they were suddenly presented with an exclusionary reality which was much broader and in urgent need of attention. Societal shifts – with people being more open about their sexual orientation, gender identity, neurodiversity, mental health, disability and religion – have also accelerated the organizational need to embrace inclusive practices.

We live in a content-driven world, which has partly driven these societal shifts. The technological changes in the last few years alone have been a lot to keep up with. Our mobile phones allow us to be connected to our external environment 24/7, and this brings many benefits but also proven detriments to our sleep and well-being. This has changed how we engage and interact socially. It has led to the emergence of individuals we now call 'influencers' and has completely disrupted industries such as marketing and recruitment, as well as making it possible for solopreneurs to do business on a large scale. We now use apps in almost every aspect of our day-to-day lives, relying on them to help us find our way around the world, do our weekly food shop, communicate with our friends and manage our finances. And every time we engage with technology in this way, it is storing our data and preferences, which is then used to behaviourally 'nudge' our choices in a slightly scary way. The cleverly designed algorithms feed us information that is of most interest to us and often that which is most aligned to our political and social views, creating a skewed view of public attitudes and increasing our perceptions of difference. All of this, to some extent, counteracts the progress we have made in recognizing some of the biases we hold, by embedding new ones that are much more covert and subtle.

In addition, the world is in a state of environmental emergency, changing forever the way we do business and our lifestyles. Most countries are in debt due to the pandemic, with significant economic instability pushing many into poverty and creating more of a divide than ever before between those living in abundance and those without. Countries are also more polarized in views than they once were, and this causes an unsettling level of tension. The future is uncertain, likely to be much different from anything we have ever experienced, and we are simultaneously being bombarded with constant change. Whilst the increasing population size may, to some, suggest a thriving world, I believe it hides a dangerous fragility. If there was ever a time for 'vigorous and positive action', as per Martin Luther King Jr's words, in the form of connectedness and togetherness, it's now.

Hitting the bottom line

There is significant research on the business case for diverse workplace representation and organizational inclusion. Yet this information doesn't always extend beyond the academic world or those who actively seek it out. Most leaders need more than encouragement that 'it's the right thing to do' – they need hard evidence that it makes business sense.

In 2020, McKinsey released their third DEI report, *Diversity Wins*. Their first analysis in 2015 found that companies in the top quartile for gender diversity in leadership teams were 15% more likely to financially outperform those in the lowest quartile, but by 2020 this had increased to 25%.[3] When it comes to the ethnic diversity of leadership teams, the difference in financial performance of companies in the top and bottom quartiles has stayed consistently high over the years at around 35%. Credit Suisse Research Institute's 2021 *Gender 3000* report adds to the longitudinal data, showing that organizations with more gender diversity at both board and C-suite levels benefit from a 'diversity premium' of increased net income over time.[4] Interestingly, they also found that having greater gender diversity offers a lower risk profile in the eyes of the credit market, leading to higher credit ratings. An above-average female representation also increased the share price performance over a 10-year period compared to companies that were below average.

As would also make logical sense, when individuals with diverse thoughts are brought together to solve problems, new and innovative ideas are more likely to come about. Professor Katherine Phillips spent her academic career researching diversity and the impact on decision-making. In a 2014 article in *Scientific American*, she explains an earlier study looking at the impact of racial diversity in small groups.[5] They put people into groups of three – some were all-White and some had two White members and one non-White member – and gave them a murder mystery exercise. All group members had some common information, and they each had important information that the other group members did not. To find out who committed the crime, they had to share all the information they collectively possessed. They found that the racially diverse groups significantly outperformed the groups with no racial diversity. Phillips explains: 'Being with similar others leads us to think we all hold the same information and share the same perspective. This perspective, which stopped the all-White groups from effectively processing the information, is what hinders creativity and innovation.' In other words, our brains are lazy, and so being with people who are different from us provokes greater thought compared to being with people who look like us. Whilst this is inevitably more uncomfortable and takes more effort and likely more time, the benefits for businesses are clear.

Of course, simply having greater diversity won't lead to positive business outcomes without an inclusive culture that embraces difference. In their *Getting to Equal 2019* report, Accenture identify how a culture of equality drives employees' innovation mindset.[6] In particular, the key driver to innovation is people feeling like they are in an 'Empowering Environment' where they are trusted and have the freedom to be creative. Naturally, with innovative leadership comes a greater ability to anticipate customer needs and preferences, leading to improved customer retention and growth. In addition, diverse thinking can spot gaps in the market, call out barriers to certain customers using products or services, and design new products to attract a wider audience. In an episode of my podcast, *Why Care?*,[7] Caroline Nankinga, previously the Global Diversity and Inclusion Lead for Pentland Brands, explained:

> Our brands are working to ensure that what we do brings more inclusion and doesn't just talk to a particular subset of our consumers. So, if I think about Speedo, there's work to be done to encourage more people from ethnic minority backgrounds to enjoy the water, whether that's thinking about protective hair products or thinking about more modest product ranges... We have a partnership with the Black Swimming Association, for example, which is really helping us learn and understand what we can do to encourage more inclusion.

As demonstrated in Caroline's example, Pentland Brands actively sought diverse perspectives and views through external partnerships in order to create products for a new customer segment, thereby growing their market.

The power of listening to and aligning products to diverse consumer needs is no better illustrated than in the 2023 redesign of the all-white England women's football team kit. After concerns raised by players about period leakage, Nike designed blue shorts with an integrated absorbent liner. Who designed the original kit? Men, I imagine. Whose voices needed to be heard to ensure it was suitable for a different customer demographic? Women. Winning the Euro 2022 tournament gave the England women's team status and offered them a voice (that warranted attention) to convey their need. Would this need have been identified otherwise? It probably would never have occurred to any of the male decision-makers to ask. It invites the question, therefore, what are more homogeneous leadership teams and organizations missing simply because of their narrower perspective on the world?

Here are a few more examples of how inclusive design can make or break a company:

o   In 2019, a British Black man submitted his photo for an online passport application. The facial recognition system rejected his photo with the comment: 'It looks like your mouth is open.' He then had to explain why he wanted to submit the photo anyway: 'My mouth is closed, I just have big lips.'[8]

o   The passport application news story offered a platform for others to share similar experiences. It was revealed that Snapchat's facial recognition filters weren't designed to identify minority ethnic features. In 2020, Snapchat released its first annual diversity report, which indicated that only 4.1% of employees over its entire workforce were Black and African American and under 7% were Hispanic and Latinx. Only 3.2% of these groups were in leadership positions.[9] It's not surprising that the algorithm had exclusionary design flaws.

o   Mattel's Barbie doll has faced significant criticism over the years for encouraging children to have an unrealistic impression of the female figure. Academics in South Australia found that girls aged five to eight who played with Barbie were more likely to think that being thin is ideal.[10] Following a 29% drop in gross sales from 2012 to 2015, Mattel overhauled the Barbie collection to focus on a more diverse range of dolls. Now available are dolls with a hearing aid or a prosthetic limb, dolls in a wheelchair and dolls with Down's syndrome, as well as dolls of different height, shape and skin tone, and dolls with a variety of careers. By 2016, Barbie sales jumped 16% compared to the previous year.[11]

o   In 2016, Airbnb faced significant criticism after Black users started sharing stories of hosts refusing their requests. Some explained that they were only able to get bookings if they changed their profile photos to images of White people.[12] The company came under further criticism in 2021 when it introduced an optional pricing algorithm, which Black hosts hesitated to use. This led to White hosts earning more than Black hosts, inadvertently widening the social inequality gap.[13] There are several reasons behind these issues, one of which is the overrepresentation of White employees. Figures for June 2022 show 39.6% of employees were White and 15% were members of underrepresented ethnic groups.[14] This means there were few technical engineers to provide a diverse racial lens and few Black, Asian or Hispanic senior decision-makers who could influence the strategy.

More often these days, tenders for new work require evidence that DEI practice has been actively embedded in the organization. Companies with corporate social responsibility high on their agendas want supply chains with equal integrity and commitment to DEI. It's interesting to observe the slight panic on people's faces when they realize they are quite far behind the DEI curve and that they may lose out on new business because they have absolutely nothing to say on the matter. This is often where the business case hits home quickly.

Slightly less tangible is the impact of DEI work on employer brand and reputation. An organization's reputation is precious and directly impacts customer buying choices, whether people recommend and speak positively about the organization and whether they want to work there. According to the Global RepTrak 100, which ranks the reputation of the world's leading companies, in 2023 reputation scores were down across all industries compared to previous years.[15] They relate this to the volatility in the market (caused by the increased cost of living, the Russian invasion of Ukraine, issues with the supply of certain goods, etc.), but also to companies not living up to post-pandemic expectations by continuing previous habits that employees no longer value.

One habit or cultural norm that has created plenty of post-pandemic debate and polarized views is office- versus home-based or hybrid working. Despite LinkedIn's *Future of Recruiting 2023* report, which highlights that hybrid working is the fastest-growing priority for candidates looking for jobs,[16] many organizations have found it challenging to create an inclusive policy on this that meets business needs. British businessman and entrepreneur Lord Alan Sugar has been quoted as saying that people who work from home are 'lazy layabouts',[17] and Elon Musk set a return to office policy requiring Tesla employees to spend a minimum of 40 hours per week in the office.[18] Who is this policy most likely to affect? People with caring responsibilities and those with a disability or illness. These types of autocratic, fixed views can severely bruise an organization's reputation, although given the size and scale of Sugar's and Musk's empires, they have the luxury of not needing to care. When Musk announced he was banning working from home at Twitter in November 2022, big brands such as General Motors, United Airlines, Deutsche Bank and Audi all paused their Twitter ads for fear of being tarnished through association, creating a huge dent in revenues. In today's world, employees, customers and investors feel so passionately about organizational responsibility in relation to DEI that many are willing to walk if they don't see that a company is doing enough or they don't feel value aligned.

Parenting and caring

I could write a subsection on every diversity category mentioned in this chapter, providing compelling reasons for better inclusion efforts for each one. For example, simply looking at the growing figures on those self-identifying as LGBTQ+, people diagnosed with mental health issues and the global neurodivergent population signposts that organizations need to do more to understand and include these individuals, who are increasingly reflected in their workforce. However, there is something unique and distinct about parenting and caring – in all countries, no matter what gender, ethnicity, sexual orientation or age one is, these are categories that most people identify with at some point in their lives. In addition, the economic impact of poor government and organizational family- and caring-friendly policies is significant. Huge numbers are falling out of the labour market due to caring responsibilities. The UK workforce participation rate is 76% of mothers compared to 92% of fathers.[19] This gap is slightly larger in the US, at 73% compared to 93%, respectively.[20] The main reasons for this gender disparity, alongside societal gender expectations, are the struggle to find affordable childcare, unempathetic and unsupportive employers, and inflexible working policies. In their 2023 Fair Growth report, the Centre for Progressive Policy show that a rise of just 1 percentage point in the gender employment gap reduces productivity by £0.06 per hour[21] – this makes a clear business case for gender equality.

Whilst globally, nuclear families (adult couples with a child or children) are still in the majority, this is on the decline. In the UK, nearly 25% of families are headed by lone parents,[22] and 32% of these lone parents are unemployed.[23] The US has the highest share of lone parent families in the world, at 23%.[24] In their 2021 research on single mothers, Dr Laura Radcliffe and colleagues highlight the overwhelming incompatibility between what it means to be a good mum and workplace pressures.[25] One single mother is quoted as saying: 'I'd absorb, absorb and absorb like a dry sponge but then I felt like I was leaking. I could take no more in; my sponge was too full and I was just collapsing… everything was oozing out because there was no more capacity.' It's no wonder that unemployed single parents might not find work an attractive prospect – it comes with significant stress, poorer mental health and likely no real financial gain, given the scale of childcare costs. It is clear that an organization which tailors support to the specific needs of single parents would easily stand out from the crowd. Not only would they avoid high turnover costs by retaining skilled and knowledgeable employees, but they would also be able to access a growing, yet hard-to-reach, talent pool of experience.

When it comes to parenting and caring, 'flexibility' is the golden word – it is the common need across all working caregivers, the job characteristic that will make them stay in an organization and the one that will attract fresh talent from this category. The post-pandemic lifestyle has led to both a desire and an expectation that organizations will offer flexible working, with 24% of all UK workers now working in a hybrid way.[26] Moreover, the modern-day dad wants to be an active and equal caregiver, which is clear in the marked upwards trend of fathers working part-time hours: 11% in 2022 compared to 4% in 2019, according to the *Working Families Index 2022* report.[27] Research by DaddiLife in 2019 shows that two-thirds of millennial (born in the period from the early 1980s to the late 1990s) dads had requested flexible working, though a very small proportion of these requests were formally granted.[28] In my interview with Han-Son Lee, Founder of DaddiLife, in 2023, he explained the tension younger fathers have with their employers: 'One father told me that his flexible working request was turned down because the policy "wasn't for dads, just for mums". Gone are the days where men are the ones just expected to work, so organizations must adapt to the needs of modern day dads.' In other words, meeting the needs of fathers in the workplace will soon be a baseline requirement, not a nice-to-have policy. Forward-thinking companies which have already put in place tailored support are now more keenly sought after. Music Football Fatherhood, founded by Elliott Rae, runs the Annual Working Dads Employers Awards.[29] Being an award-winner on such a list or any other list that commends inclusive organizational practices is a highly effective and low-cost tool for attracting talent.

Transitioning back to work after having a period of time off is tough, particularly if you are a first-time parent – you have to get your head around any workplace changes that happened when you were away, get used to leaving your child with someone else, learn to juggle work and caring responsibilities and, if there's time amongst all of that, find your new norm. In an early episode of my podcast, I spoke to DEI changemaker and entrepreneur Sophie Smallwood, and we discussed our experiences of being a first-time mother. I explained how I felt I needed to prove that I was still just as career-focused for fear my employer would think I wasn't as committed as I had been (in fact, I returned to a position two grades lower than when I had left... but that's another story). Sophie shared how she missed the 'cerebral stimulation' of work and would have returned from maternity leave sooner if there had been a more flexible return option on offer. But I have also heard stories that are the complete opposite, with parents only returning to work because they really have to, their hearts and minds still being with their children. The risk is that without considerable support wrapped around each person and their individual needs, the risks of low productivity, mental health challenges and falling out of the workplace entirely are high – and costly to us all.

Given that the majority of the workforce is parenting and caring in some way, embedding inclusive, family-friendly practices is one of the best ways for organizations to guarantee they will attract the best talent, retain healthy and fulfilled employees, enhance employer brand and, ultimately, have a higher chance of longevity.

The next generations

Organizational culture is grounded in history and maintained by the people at the top, who are often (not always) of an older generation. We are currently seeing the tail end of the baby boomer generation (born around the mid-1940s up to the mid-1960s) in the workplace. In many organizations, these individuals sit in positions of power, perhaps as C-suite directors, non-executives or investors. These are post-Great Depression and post-World War II babies, who lived through the Cold War and the Vietnam War and were pioneers for civil rights. As such, they have a strong work ethic, viewing success as getting a promotion and placing weight on being able to pay their way and provide for their families. With retirement age being continuously extended in countries around the world, we are now seeing a unique situation where four generations are of working age at the same time.

Born in the period from the late 1990s to the early 2010s, Generation Z will constitute about 27% of our workforce by 2025.[30] They are the first generation never to have known a world without the internet or mobile phones, and they are baffled when they find floppy discs lying at the bottom of their parents' desk drawers. According to Deloitte's *Welcome to Generation Z* report, which is based on 2018 data, they tend to view salary as less important than previous generations and are much more socially and environmentally driven.[31] The report also explains that diversity is one of their top priorities, and they are looking for employers to be actively and visibly supporting representation across all characteristics, including gender identity and sexual orientation. In addition, they don't see their career in the form of a ladder, starting at the bottom and gradually working their way to the top. Gen Z want a personalized career experience, gathering a variety of skills and experience in a more lattice-style approach to career progression. With this picture in mind, you can see how this generation might be viewed as 'lacking commitment', 'irresponsible' and 'entitled' by the baby boomer generation, who, at that age, were 'grateful for what they got' and weren't afraid of 'hard graft'. In return, Gen Z feel frustrated at having to comply with a fixed-formula workplace culture that doesn't fulfil their needs.

Whilst not everyone in each generation will act and feel the same, these general perspectives nevertheless underpin a valuable point in the DEI business case. Unless those at the top are willing to step away from their belief system and embrace an inclusive mindset by taking Gen Z's perspective on work into account, this younger generation are quite prepared to exit via the nearest escape route and find somewhere that will. Senior leaders may find this shift of power in the employer–employee contract unsettling. They can choose to sit with this discomfort and seek to redesign the workplace so it is appealing to future generations, thereby creating an environment that could well be at odds with how they want their organization to be. Or they can maintain that in order to effectively serve customers, jobs need to be delivered the way they have always have been, but they must acknowledge the loss of talent as a result. According to a 2019 report by the Workforce Institute, 33% of Gen Z workers wouldn't tolerate an employer that didn't give them any say over their work schedule, and one in four would work harder for a company that supported them to work the way they wanted to.[32] This suggests the claim that Gen Z are less motivated and committed is a false accusation, as they will demonstrate a strong work ethic if they feel seen, heard and listened to.

I believe that continuous analysis of the future through a DEI lens, and flexing to meet the changing demands, will be organizations' greatest asset. Short-sightedness has been the downfall of an endless number of companies that chose to stick with the status quo. Kodak's denial of the disruption of digital photography meant it was far too late to pivot when they realized the market had changed. Video-rental chain Blockbuster turned down the opportunity to buy Netflix in 2000 and realized four years too late that online film subscription was the way to go.[33] Blackberry stuck rigidly to its keyboard when Apple innovated with touchscreen, failing to adapt to consumers' need for more user-friendly, responsive devices. When you read the back stories of these companies, there was always a voice around the table expressing change in consumer trends and urging a review of the product or service, but regretfully this was ignored in these cases. Let's face it, it always feels safer and less risky to stick with what we know even though it may be false confidence to think that it will continue to serve us in the future. In a similar way, senior leaders would be living in a fairy tale if they thought Gen Z's workplace requirements are merely a blip in generational norms and the world will soon revert to the work ethic of the past. Indeed, Generation Alpha (born after Gen Z) are set to be a hyper version of Gen Z. Spending their formative years during the global pandemic, they are even more family focused and more attuned to the well-being of the planet and fellow humans, and they have an intrinsic need for inclusion, belonging and representation.[34] Organizations ignore this at their peril.

The future of work

We are living in a world where advancement in technology has disrupted the marketplace – the smartphone in the communications, music and photography industries, cloud services in the data storage industry, chatbots in the customer services industry, on-demand TV in the entertainment industry and virtual reality in the gaming and training industries, to name a few. With the emergence of ChatGPT, robotics and other artificial intelligence advancements, more repetitive tasks will be automated and the need for expert knowledge and advice will be reduced. Waiting in the wings to further disrupt are self-driving cars and drones, 5G and further development of the Internet of Things, industrial automation, smart cities and quantum computing, all of which will accelerate our ability to solve problems and make decisions at the blink of an eye. With this speed of change, the *Future of Jobs 2023* report by the World Economic Forum predicts that in five years, 44% of workers will have to gain new skills and there will be a loss of 83 million jobs.[35] The jobs that are more likely to disappear are lower-paid manual and clerical jobs and those that involve repetitive tasks. The risk, from a DEI perspective, is that this will extend the socio-economic divide even more unless we find a way to reskill these workers.

However, it's by no means all bad news. There will be new job growth and opportunities on an individual level to rapidly upskill and pivot to emerging market needs. On a macro level, organizations will need creative and diverse thinking more than ever to evolve with the marketplace and remain relevant. Leaders will continuously need to make rapid and tough decisions about the future of their organizations, shifting strategic focus, automating where possible, streamlining for efficiencies and upskilling in new areas. Critically, throughout this, there will be a need for care, empathy, active listening and inclusive leadership to maintain a positive workplace culture. This will be no mean feat given the vulnerability and fear that will naturally be experienced by employees in such a turbulent and unsettling time. They will need leaders who can support their agility, develop their curiosity for the possibility of change and build their motivation for lifelong learning. I strongly believe that through all the redundancies, technological disruption, environmental threats and political turmoil ahead, organizations that lead with care and support for their employees' unique needs will prevail.

So, how does this relate to DEI? I'll explain using as a metaphor my two-year-old daughter's love for stacking LEGO bricks as high as they will go. I watch her continue to place one block directly on top of the other until the tower is much taller than she is. At a certain point, it starts to lean slightly under the weight – this is her moment to shine, and as she reaches out with one small finger and taps, so it comes crashing to the ground. She squeals with delight and starts the whole building process again. The issue with her engineering of course (although we shall forgive her as she is only two after all) is that the foundation of the tower is just a single brick at the bottom. And this is the predicament that organizations are finding themselves in now. Having spent little or no time investing in DEI or building inclusive leadership capacity, they are finding themselves on very rocky ground. Cracks have formed where underrepresented groups are now voicing their experiences of exclusion and discrimination in the workplace, mistakes have made it into the public domain, and the general sense of belonging is poor. Faced with everything we know about the future of work, this fragility is extremely concerning. The unity and solidarity that inclusion and belonging bring is what will offer organizations the strength to navigate through the current and impending disruptions. If they do not have this foundation, they will buckle under the weight of one disruption too many. Should this happen, the only ones squealing with delight will be their competitors.

Chapter summary

In this chapter, I offered a macro perspective of the world as we experience it today and explained how DEI is intricately linked to every aspect of our daily lives. The emergence of DEI has been accelerated by events such as the global pandemic, societal changes in relation to previously taboo subjects, and technological advances which have disrupted industries whilst also revealing discriminatory design flaws. With the current economic state of the world, the environmental crisis and the considerable turmoil and uncertainty that continues to unfold around us, there is greater urgency than ever to focus on inclusion. However, the reasons why aren't always obvious.

I shared the positive impact of diversity on financial turnover, problem-solving, innovation and employer brand. I also articulated the business case for inclusion, using examples of parents and carers as well as the younger generations. These groups make up a significant proportion of the workforce and are highly influential in steering the course of the future of work. Paying attention to their values and needs, as well as those of other underrepresented groups, and creating strength through togetherness will be what determines which organizations survive and thrive.

Questions of discomfort

You may not have needed this chapter to offer sound reasoning as to why DEI is vital to your organization, but I hope, if nothing else, it has been a fascinating and thought-provoking read. It might even have prompted insightful conversation over dinner with friends. It's probably worth saying at this stage, though, that as you move Beyond Discomfort in your role as an inclusive leader, there will be times when both your head and your heart will need a timely reminder as to why this work is important. So, feel free to use this chapter as an aide-memoir or indeed to help you articulate the case for change to anyone who may need to hear it.

Here are a few questions to provoke further thought:

o   How is inclusion experienced in your organization, and how does that experience differ depending on people's diversity characteristics? How do you know that's the case? How can you find out more?

o   What does your current external brand and reputation suggest regarding DEI? If potential employees were to search for your company online, what would they find about your approach to DEI on your website, in the news, on social media channels, etc.? What impression would they be left with?

o   What is your organization's policy on hybrid or home working? Who contributed to designing the policy? How flexible or fixed is this, and does the same apply in all departments or teams? If not, is there clear rationale why?

o   How do people with different caring responsibilities experience working in your organization? Are managers equipped with the knowledge and skills they need to effectively tailor their approach based on individual needs?

o   What is the generational make-up of your organization? In what ways might generational exclusion be experienced? How can you tap into the mindset of younger employees to help redesign for the future?

o   To what extent does the future of work and the implications for your organization come up in regular discussions? What DEI work needs to take place to create a stronger, more resilient foundation for your organization?

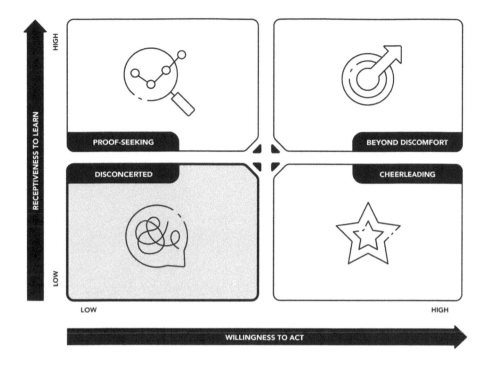

RECEPTIVENESS TO LEARN

HIGH

LOW

PROOF-SEEKING

BEYOND DISCOMFORT

DISCONCERTED

CHEERLEADING

LOW

HIGH

WILLINGNESS TO ACT

2 Disconcerted

> Neuroscientists have found that when your core ideas, identities, ideologies
> are attacked, you actually respond in a similar way to pain. So, it feels like
> you're being punched in the mind and you immediately put your guard up.
> —Adam Grant, psychologist and author[1]

We've all come across plenty of two-by-two models and we know that
the bottom left-hand corner ('low, low') is usually far from desirable. It
tends to represent the least-favoured option, or the one that you should
put least resources into, as it gives little return. That is not the case with
the Beyond Discomfort® model – having a primarily Disconcerted Way
of Being when it comes to DEI does not say anything about your ethics
or integrity as a human. As you read this chapter, I'd encourage you to
set aside your existing understanding of two-by-two models and try to

be less interested in the position of the box and focus more on whether the values and beliefs resonate and whether you recognize any of the associated emotions.

In this chapter, I discuss why DEI can seem unfair, unpack the concept of privilege and the fallacy behind our beliefs about meritocracy. I also highlight two fears that provoke discomfort in those with a Disconcerted Way of Being and offer guidance on how to navigate these.

It isn't fair

Like many people, I have been enthralled by the HBO series *The White Lotus*. The first season is about the stories that unfold for guests staying at a fictitious hotel in Hawaii. If you haven't seen it, it's well worth a watch. Aside from the captivating storyline, the writers have done a superb job of interweaving themes of social injustice and inequity throughout. There is a particular scene that, for me, captures the essence of Disconcerted when one of the straight, White, male characters says:

> For years, I was the good guy, you know? I was the one in the room, saying, like, 'Hey, that's not cool', to all the chauvinists and bigots. But now I'm the bad guy, or at least, I shouldn't say anything on account of my inherited traits. I mean, why do I need to prove my anti-racist bona fides? It seems wrong.

Let's look at the emotions behind these words. I hear the character's hurt, confusion and feelings of being criticized and under attack based on his majority-group diversity characteristics, which he has no control over. That seems unfair and unjust. And he also feels under pressure to actively demonstrate he is pro inclusion. What he is observing is that people like him don't have legitimacy to comment on matters of diversity and inclusion anymore – that he is outside the conversation (something we'll come back to later on in the chapter).

And this goes hand in hand with a deep concern that anyone who identifies with majority-group characteristics are being actively overlooked for jobs and discriminated against because of their background. In a workshop I facilitated in 2022, a White, female participant took this view:

> I fear that the pendulum might have swung the other way now. I mean I'm a momma-bear of three blue-eyed, blonde-haired White boys, and I want to protect them. If we put more effort into minorities, I mean, would it put us in a better place? It's not what's on the outside but what's between the ears.

I have heard this belief that the pendulum has swung too far in the opposite direction on many occasions. When delving deeper, it is usually the absence of male-only development programmes and the feeling that there aren't any opportunities available specifically for that group that is the issue. This doesn't seem fair when there are talent programmes specifically for women, people in minority ethnic groups or those with other underrepresented characteristics. The feeling of being left out and excluded is both hurtful and frustrating.

Those who are Disconcerted believe that fairness exists when everyone is treated in exactly the same way. However, this assumes that the world already operates according to this principle. What we often don't see is the daily adaptations that people from underrepresented groups make to fit in, or how the world treats them because of their difference. In my podcast conversation with DEI leader Rukasana Bhaijee, I learnt about her experience as a South Asian, Muslim girl growing up in England in the 1980s. She described the challenges of living in a British culture whilst navigating her South Asian cultural norms: 'It was almost like toggling two worlds or two operating systems. So it literally was operating like an Apple iOS and an Android.' She explained how rare it was to see someone of her cultural background on TV and how people would stare if she wore her South Asian clothing. At the age of 17, she stopped wearing her traditional *shalwar kameez* in public places, because she was so keen to integrate and fit in. She also shared her story of reclaiming her Muslim identity and wearing a hijab later on in life. However, in doing so, she opened herself up to microaggressions and inequity.

> After kids, I retrained as a complementary therapist and got a Saturday job. I had to go through 21 interviews in many different organizations. People were calling me for interview based on the qualifications on my résumé. But as soon as I entered a space, the visible response from some folks was one of shock. And I guess when you close your eyes and picture a complementary therapist, a short Asian woman in a hijab maybe doesn't come to mind straight away. So, they would see me and pretty much within the first minute of the conversation, I would know that this wasn't going anywhere. It was then that I really realized, as a South Asian woman, I experienced otherness, I experienced maybe even curiosity, in some cases, discrimination, but now I felt like an outsider in a completely different way.

In another podcast conversation, Christina Brooks, a woman of Black British heritage and Founder and CEO of diverse talent attraction agency Ruebik, offered a similar story:

> Early on, in my head-hunting career, I remember going to meet an investment banker (I used to place investment bankers and private equity professionals into roles across the city). And as I walked in and sat at his table, he took one look at me and stood up and walked away, walked out. That was purely because of the colour of my skin, because we'd had several conversations on the phone, and he would not have known my heritage.

Rukasana's and Christina's stories shine a light on the specific challenges that people of different cultural backgrounds face living in a culture where their 'face doesn't fit' the norm. Rukasana expressed the cognitive load this presents and the emotional drain of not belonging. Their stories also illustrate that despite what is 'between the ears', what's on the outside does matter – a lot.

Dealing with individuals' unmet needs

Let's assume you have a DEI programme in your organization that focuses on minority ethnic employees. It's important not to ignore comments about people feeling excluded from the DEI work and development programmes in your organization.

Firstly, make sure you have the data to back up why you are focusing on certain groups of people over others and check for yourself that you have a good justification for this. You need to demonstrate that it isn't about preventing White men (or other majority groups) from developing their roles, but you also need to deal with the fear or concern that comes from being left out and feeling that others are being given an unfair advantage. Whilst this process may provoke feelings of annoyance and frustration for some, it's important that all colleagues feel like their challenges have been listened to and heard. Equally, as a leader, you should help facilitate thinking through open questions that allow individuals to notice what their unmet need actually is.

Secondly, keep reinforcing that DEI is about everyone. If people feel excluded in some way and feel that they can't show up to work being true to who they are, then the organization needs to better understand what is culturally driving their experience so measures can be put in place to address the problem.

Thirdly, where there are conversations taking place in the organization amongst people with specific diversity characteristics, such as in a women's network, a race network or other employee resource groups, make sure it's clear that this is inclusive of allies – that is, those who don't personally identify with the group but want to show their support.

Meritocracy... or mirrortocracy

To compensate for the bias and discrimination that people encounter if their face doesn't fit the norm, several organizations have taken positive action by setting quotas or clear targets to create parity of representation, particularly at senior levels. Whether formal quotas have been set or simply overt intentions have been communicated for greater representation, it often leaves people in the majority group feeling like they have less chance than before of getting a job or progressing in an organization. And that also seems unfair and often creates a feeling of resentment, with individuals feeling they need to defend what they have worked for. Leaders who tend to struggle the most with positive action have a fundamental belief in the concept of meritocracy – they consider workplaces to be fair and their success as due to their own hard work alone. What they have observed and experienced in the world has never indicated otherwise. Indeed, how could we ever quantify how much of their career success was down to hard work, ability and talent versus the positive bias deep in the system that favours people who look and speak like them?

On my podcast, when I spoke to Kristen Anderson, CEO and board member at European Women on Boards and former Chief Diversity & Inclusion Officer at Barilla, she helped unpick this complexity:

There's the effect of what I call *mirrortocracy* instead of *meritocracy*. A lot of people say 'I don't believe in quotas or targets because I believe in meritocracy', meaning 'I believe that we should promote or bring on board the most qualified people.' But let's be very clear, meritocracy is a wonderful theory, but it is not reality, because that means we have no biases. If I can evaluate every single candidate without any biases coming into my evaluation, I'm following meritocracy. But we're not robots and we do have biases. We tend to have an affinity bias – mirrortocracy. For example, I want to bring Kath on because she reminds me of myself when I was more junior in my career and I think she is the right person for the leadership team. I don't realize I have this bias, and so I'm not considering Luca, who is actually a more qualified candidate.

Let's take a closer look at what we mean by 'affinity bias'. Imagine entering a large conference room full of several hundred people. You stand by the entranceway alone for several minutes observing the small groups of people having intimate discussions with a drink in one hand and a small plate of canapés in the other, which are impossible to eat without a third hand. You continue scanning in the hope that perhaps you'll spot a familiar face or even someone who might offer a friendly smile and invitation to join.

Ever found yourself in this situation? What you're less conscious of in those moments is the filtering your brain is doing to decide who to approach. Purely based on how someone looks, how they're standing and what they're wearing, you are making an instant assessment of how sociable they are, how appealing the conversation might be and whether you will have something in common. The risk, if you get this wrong, is that you'll be stuck in dull conversation for the rest of the day or, worse, discussing issues with someone you don't agree with.

There's nothing fundamentally wrong with a desire to be with someone who is comfortable and easy to talk to or work with. Why would you deliberately choose to spend the day with someone who is irritating because they have different views to you or someone who you need to expend a lot of energy on when you're in their presence? Ultimately, it's our basic instinct of self-protection that kicks in. However, if we remain open to accepting that we have this tendency to be attracted to people similar to us, and that this influences our decision-making, then it does call into question whether we achieved our promotions and job successes purely on the basis of talent alone. What if people have chosen you because you were similar to them? That's a pretty hard pill to swallow, right?

When I interviewed Jen (anonymized) in 2022, she so clearly described the impact of affinity bias at a team level, drawing on the story of a past manager:

> He had this combination of being a micromanager but also a perfectionist, and so we had to read his mind about how to do something. If we hadn't read his mind correctly, we would be punished, and he would look at every detail, which resulted in him being able to work with only a handful of people and really alienating anyone who thought slightly differently from him. So, it was extremely exclusionary. And he basically created an army of mini-hims to get the work done.

Affinity bias is covert and deeply embedded in organizational systems, and it often only becomes visible when an organization's diversity make-up is examined. In a workshop for a global client in 2022, I observed the following discussion between participants about the lack of leadership diversity.

'I have noticed that nearly all the leaders in this company are Caucasian, even those who lead the Asian teams', one participant shared.

Then came an offer from their colleague to help rationalize why this might be the case: 'Western leaders might be leading Asian teams to make sure that people aren't working 14-hour days, like they are culturally expected to – so they are there to instil the organizational culture.'

This was followed by an alternative rationale from another participant: 'Or perhaps the organization only sees good leaders as having characteristics similar to those from Western cultures?'

With these differing possibilities, complex systems and affinity bias mind traps, it's worth asking yourself a few questions to uncover why you think there were predominantly White leaders in regions where the majority are not White. What rationale do you lean towards? What rationale makes you feel the most discomfort? And, most importantly, what are the reasons for your response?

The dirty word: privilege

I have been taken aback on a number of occasions in relation to how the word 'privilege' lands with people. By definition, this is a right or advantage that only a small number of people have, and it jars with people, especially when the word 'White' or 'male' is placed before it. The emotion is there immediately, and whilst they don't articulate their point in so many words, what I am sure they want to shout out is something like:

> *How dare you tell me that I haven't had to work to get to where I am, that I've had an easy life! I grew up in a poor household. I was bullied for wearing clothes that were handed down from my three older brothers and never really fit properly. I know what it feels like to be excluded, and I have made my way despite that.*

It's understandable that by suggesting someone has privilege, it feels like we're diminishing their success, and that cuts deep at their pride. By default, if they have had an advantage, that means other people have been disadvantaged, and both of these positions are invisible and impossible to measure. When I spoke to Shawna Ferguson, Senior Managing Director at Wellington Management, on my podcast, she offered an analogy: 'Sometimes when people say *"Well, I just wish all of these underrepresented groups would lift themselves up like our forefathers pulled themselves up by their bootstraps"*... Well, that's really hard to do if you don't have boots.' Of course, one could argue that if privilege was as tangible as shoes are, then it would certainly be less disputable. As a minority ethnic woman, how could I ever know how much harder I had to work to achieve the successes in my career compared to my White, male counterparts? Or indeed, if I had to work harder at all?

What is insightful about Shawna's boot analogy is that it references an assumption we tend to carry with us as we walk through the world – that other people's experience of the world is the same as ours. So, if people apply grit and work hard as we have done, then they will reap the same rewards. Systems psychologist David Kantor explains that this assumption fails to consider the 'invisible reality' within the privacy of each person's mind.[2] In other words, our interpretation of what we see and hear is based on our own unique lens, past experiences, biases and flaws. We naturally don't have access to other people's invisible realities, but they are always present and always inform our relationships, what we communicate and our outcomes. When entering a conversation about privilege, we're asking people to accept that what they observe in the world, and therefore what is true to them, is no one else's truth but their own. It might come very close to someone else's truth, which is more likely to be the case if they share similar diversity characteristics and a similar cultural lens. But because of our unique invisible realities, it'll never be 100% the same. This makes privilege hard to identify.

When I was pregnant with our second daughter, my husband and I decided it was time for a slightly bigger car. After a lot of research, we were ready to purchase and booked an appointment at the dealership. We sat for an hour with the young, White, male sales consultant, who talked us through all the information about the specification, finance agreement and optional extras. The whole time, however, he made no eye contact with me. Even when I asked a question, he still directed his answer towards my husband. After about 45 minutes of this, I grew impatient and frustrated. In as calm a voice as I could muster, I enquired whether he realized that he hadn't looked at or spoken to me the whole time we were there. Both my husband and sales consultant paused, oblivious to what had been playing out. I could feel the discomfort that I had created as a result of calling out the sales consultant's bias. It looked like neither of them could breathe for a second or two. The sales consultant awkwardly apologized and explained that this hadn't been his intention, and the conversation continued with him consciously making an effort to direct his attention to both of us.

There were two people in that interaction, aside from me, who could have noticed the exclusionary behaviour. We wouldn't necessarily expect the sales consultant to realize, unless he was being deliberate in his actions. So, what was the reason my husband didn't pick up on it? His privilege of being a straight, White man means that he has never directly experienced being excluded in this way. And because of this, he just wasn't aware that it was something that happened to other people and so he wasn't looking for it. Just to clarify, this is not his fault; nor is it anyone else's fault that they have privilege. We can't be blamed or made to feel guilty for our background, skin colour or gender, or for not experiencing every type of exclusion that exists. That expectation is neither right nor fair. However, once a leader is aware of a form of exclusionary behaviour, it is absolutely their responsibility to be alert to it and take action when they see it.

In July 2020, West Indies cricket commentator Michael Holding offered further insight on privilege as the absence of an experience:

> I don't see any White people going into a store on Oxford Street and being followed. A Black man walks in, someone is following him everywhere he goes. That is basic White privilege. Whether a White person is there to rob the store or not, they are not going to be thought of in that way.[3]

A further example, this time of male privilege, is the general absence of people commenting on what men are wearing, their hairstyle or whether they've gained or lost weight. This is illustrated well by press commentary on female political leaders' choice of attire, which has on many occasions completely distracted from what they were saying. There was a huge uproar when former Prime Minister Theresa May was photographed wearing leather trousers 'at her age', and Hillary Clinton was criticized for 'dressing a like a flag' when she wore red, white and blue. You only have to search online for 'Angela Merkel clothes' to see the dozens of articles about her fashion decisions and faux pas. Of course, there are male politicians who have deliberately attracted attention to their looks – Donald Trump and Boris Johnson to name a couple – the difference being that they have used their appearance as a way to command greater power. However, for the most part, men can walk into a room without their looks being equated to their worth.

Let's pause a moment for an internal scan of what you're thinking and feeling after reading about these examples of disparity and inequity. What do you notice in yourself in reading these examples of privilege? Are you curious and wanting to explore what might be absent in your experiences of the world? Are you reflective about how your privilege may have influenced how people respond to you? Are you feeling frustrated or defensive, and if so, what has triggered this in you?

A note on privilege

There is some nuance to privilege that is less spoken about. Privilege is socially constructed and therefore determined by society. At its very roots are the stereotypes and expectations we place on different groups of people. For example, in many countries, it is still expected that men will earn the money and provide for their children and women will look after the children and household. This is partly the reason why, when women enter the male domain of the workplace, they face more difficulties navigating their way up the organization. Of course, the same is true of men when they enter a female domain. Think of a father with his young child joining a parent and toddler class, for example. He may have all the characteristics of a privileged group, but he isn't in the majority in this particular context. The people who have the power here are women.

Naturally, then, as societal views have evolved over time, privilege has changed. If we look back across history, there have been numerous notable figures and movements that accelerated a shift in privilege – examples include the suffragettes, Rosa Parks, the Stonewall riots, Nelson Mandela and the 2020 resurgence of Black Lives Matter. These are huge moments in time which saw a step change in awareness, perception and beliefs, demonstrating that group privilege is malleable, based on societal changes.

Privilege can also be gained or lost at an individual level. For example, if you assessed me according to just my diversity characteristics, you might assume that the intersectionality of my gender, ethnicity, socio-economic background and being first-generation UK-born would mean I lack privilege. And to some extent you could be right. However, after (often unwillingly) being tutored and coached by my mum, I passed my primary school tests and got into a selective all-girls school. There, I sat as a minority amongst a sea of White, middle-class girls, but with the privilege of receiving the same quality of education as them.

So, if we're saying that our personal privilege can be gained over time, that also means it can be lost too. I see it as a continuum where you can move up and down depending on personal life choices. For example, I gained privilege (not consciously) through my choice of life partner – a White, middle-class man. But when he took my surname, he lost privilege. My husband now has the lifelong, painstaking task of correcting people when they misspell or mispronounce his surname! But there are other implications too. Research in 2003 by Marianne Bertrand of the University of Chicago and Sendhil Mullainathan of the Massachusetts Institute of Technology found that applicants with White-sounding names were 50% more likely to be contacted for job interviews than those with typical Black names.[4]

 The privilege continuum activity

You may wish to do this exercise individually to aid your self-understanding or with your team to generate discussion. Draw a horizontal timeline of your life and reflect on the privileges you have gained or lost. You should plot key moments when you gained privilege above the line and moments or decisions when you lost privilege below the line. I offer a fictional example in the diagram.

This can be a useful exercise to help diffuse any tension or grievance that colleagues with majority characteristics might have about being told they have privilege. It normalizes that we all have it, and that it is fluid. Reflect on your continuum – what aspects of your privilege can you control, and what is outside your control?

Example Privilege Continuum

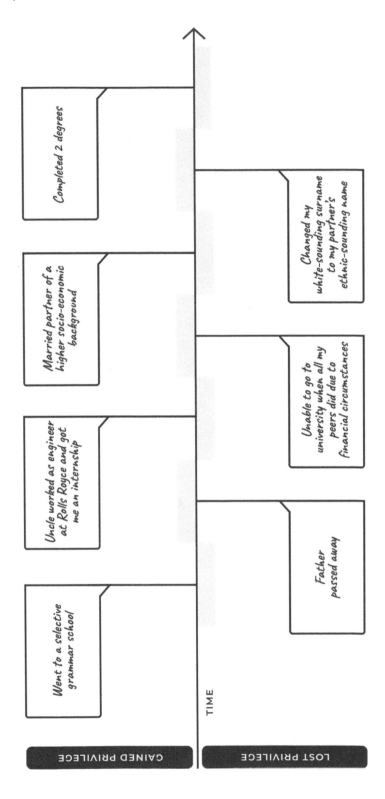

Fear of acknowledging privilege

A few years back, I was brought in as a lead facilitator for the rollout of a global leadership development programme, as an associate on behalf of another consultancy. The day before one of the scheduled programmes was due to go ahead, I was chatting to my co-facilitator – a seasoned White, male colleague – talking him through the programme as it was his first time working for this client. In passing, he referred to the day rate that the consultancy was paying him, and I tried to cover my surprise at the figure. I certainly wasn't being paid as much as him – the calculator in fact told me later that I was being paid about a third less!

After pondering what to do, I felt I couldn't just sit by and let this inequality play out – why was he on a higher rate when I was doing more work? To me, it seemed like they were paying us based on what they thought we would accept as a fair day rate, rather than on the role we were playing or on our worth. And it really hurt – I felt used, taken for granted and stupid for accepting such a low rate. So I picked up the phone and constructively challenged my contact at the consultancy, who awkwardly fudged an answer and said she would look into it in more detail.

On the first evening before the programme started, my co-facilitator and I met for dinner. I wanted him to know what I had discovered so he could share my sense of injustice. But that didn't happen. As soon as I told him that I had spoken to the consultancy, his face changed to annoyance and he said he wished I had spoken to him first. I was confused – why was he upset? Surely he could see how unfair it was? He said that he had been where they are and that it goes against etiquette for associates to discuss their day rates. He thought that my comments could affect the client's trust in him and how much work he would get from them in the future.

Let's unpack his Disconcerted Way of Being and why I didn't get the response I was hoping for. His words suggest that he was very aware of the inequitable power structures in the consultancy industry, namely that they pay associates based on a combination of experience, how much they are charging their client and how much they believe the associate is willing to accept. The fact that there is an unspoken rule not to share your day rate confirms that everyone knows the system is unfair. So, what was behind the response I got? My guess is fear, at least in part. Fear that if he acknowledges that I have been unfairly treated, then it means he has been given preferential treatment. Fear that if he overtly confirms the system is inequitable, then he admits he has colluded to keep it that way in favour of those like him who benefit. Fear that if he acknowledges his privilege, then what does that say about the worth he has placed on himself based on what others have valued him at? Fear of how the system (in this case, the consultancy) that promotes inequity will respond if he challenges it. You can see, then, why my hope for gallant camaraderie to fight the good fight was somewhat optimistic.

Just as it is hard for people in majority groups to accept they have privilege, it should be noted that it can be hard for people in minority groups to acknowledge that their background and identity influences their outcomes. I can certainly relate to this – I was bullied at school for the colour of my skin and I learnt very quickly that having brown skin wasn't a good thing. So, every day I pushed that part of my identity away. I figured I needed to embrace White British culture as much as I could in order to fit in. As a child, I remember complaining to my parents about always having rice, pulses and curries for dinner when all my friends where eating chicken nuggets and chips. I tried as best I could to ignore being in the minority for the colour of my skin, and I did it so well that by the time I got to my early twenties, as strange as it sounds, I had almost forgotten I had brown skin at all. I desperately wanted to believe that if I worked hard and did a great job, I would carve a successful career path, and therefore my ethnicity was irrelevant. I later discovered that there is a (derogatory) term for this, which is 'coconut' – that is, brown on the outside, white on the inside. Whilst it may sound like it was my choice to relinquish my Mauritian heritage in favour of White British culture, one could question the impact on my life if I hadn't.

Compared to those with majority characteristics, I find that people from underrepresented groups are more conscious of their identity and difference, often wishing that they could be parted from the labels that are placed on them so they can know for sure that their successes and failures are due to their talent alone. A female participant in one of my workshops in 2022 expressed this sentiment from a gender perspective:

> We all have our baggage, but I don't want to be lumped into the 'woman' category – that's not what I lead with and I haven't let it hold me back. It's like someone with a disability – you can't treat everyone with a disability like they can't do things if that person is not defined by it and doesn't let it hold them back.

Interestingly, the fear here is related to the desire to believe in meritocracy. It's a response against feeling like the token hire – a fear that she hasn't earned her success through her capability but because she helped her organization with its diversity statistics. Ultimately, this is a fear that eats away at her sense of self-worth.

The discomfort in acknowledging privilege exists can therefore be present for anyone – whether in majority or minority groups. By denying it, we further cement the power and inequity in our organizational systems. It's the equivalent of looking the other way when we walk past a homeless person on the street who is asking for money. Take a moment to ask yourself: when might you have looked the other way when discovering a privilege? This may be a tough question if, like me, you had done such a good job of ignoring it that you had not acknowledged it before.

Fear of change

Have you ever been tempted to say 'It wasn't like that in my day'? For those of you of a younger generation, perhaps this phrase isn't familiar to you yet, but it definitely will be at some point. When growing up in the 1980s, I remember waking up in the morning and having to wait patiently for the TV programmes to start airing. There were only four channels, no on-demand and no ability to record, so if I missed my favourite shows, I missed out. Whilst I appreciate the huge amount of content and entertainment readily available today, there is always a trade-off we make with progress. When I look at my nine-year old daughter and her peers, I see that they just have to think of something they want and there is generally a way for them to access it quickly. I look fondly back at the times before these technological developments and worry about whether our children have lost the capacity for patience or using their imagination to keep themselves occupied.

To put some of this reminiscing into context, what is being observed in the present is in the context of what has been experienced in the past. It's a comparison our brains automatically make – our past acts as a reference point for the future. Someone who is Disconcerted might remember a time when they could act freely, where they weren't conscious that what they said or did would be attributed to their diversity characteristics. So comes the sense of loss, along with frustration and confusion. What used to be acceptable – for example, challenging an inappropriate racial comment – is now potentially frowned upon as White saviourism. For those in this category who are men, should they open the door for a female colleague, or will she view it as a sign that she isn't capable of doing it by herself? There's a seemingly endless list of potential pitfalls. A fear of change is brought about by the anticipation of further changes ahead. Whilst having a particular combination of diversity characteristics may not be flavour of the month right now, with continued focus on DEI, what the Disconcerted person can see on the horizon is far worse.

In my interview with Victoria (anonymized), a public sector leader, in 2022, she offered an example to highlight this Disconcerted Way of Being:

> My new colleagues were all of Indian heritage and I was the only White person. That has never happened to me before – I had only ever worked in teams where I was in the majority. I would walk into our team meeting and they would suddenly stop talking in their own language, pause and look at me. I felt really disconnected, like I didn't belong in that team, and it was the first time I had felt that way. It felt uncomfortable and I didn't enjoy it. So, in complete honesty, if creating a more diverse and inclusive workplace means I will have to experience that more often, then I'm not sure I want that.

And there it is – the raw truth. This is a perfect example of what psychologist and author Dr Pippa Grange says is the fear of abandonment, rejection or being isolated.[5] Ironically, in Victoria's case, this fear is experienced by someone who has less experience of exclusion – even so, they know it isn't a pleasant place to be. Self-protection is part of human nature, so if this is a sentiment you share, then you should simply acknowledge it is present and be curious about where it comes from, rather than being concerned or guilty.

Just like most of us revel in the feeling of grabbing a bargain, we also enjoy any advantages we have been offered (whether earned on not) in our lives. It's what we know, and it makes for a good life and we don't want to readily give it up. The sort of question that often arises is: 'Does creating equity mean that I have to step down from my senior position, stop going on nice holidays, move into basic accommodation and give away my money?' The fear of change stems from the uncertainty of what it means for us and what it will bring, and to bring it back to an earlier reference, it cuts right at the heart of our hierarchy of needs – our need to feel safe and secure.

Part of this fear is based on a zero-sum mindset, meaning that if someone is to prosper, someone else has to miss out – that is, what do I need to give up if we achieve DEI? This suggests that people in majority groups have gained their successes purely as a result of taking away from those in the minority, and so, in order to rebalance, we need to do the reverse. The issue with this reasoning, however, is that it depicts success in a fixed and absolute way. When speaking on the Why Care? podcast to global DEI leader Sámi Ben-Ali, he explained the anxiety provoked when his organization communicated their 10-year target of 40% female leaders:

> One male leader said to me: 'By my calculations, that means 90 roles now need to go to females.' And so straight away he was looking at what exists now and replacing it. So, the conversation I had was: 'Well, think about the mindset of why does it have to mean replacement? Why can it not mean growth?'

A fair challenge. As humans, we seem to automatically jump to the negative repercussions of change because it is taking us away from what we know. It's known as the 'status quo bias', which favours keeping things as they are rather than expending energy working out what change looks like. Yet, we have all experienced situations where a seemingly adverse situation has led to new opportunities and a positive change. Rather than viewing success as a fixed quantity that needs to be divided up, perhaps we can imagine success as something that can be cultivated and grown exponentially so that there is plenty for all.

If this discussion on giving up something for the sake of DEI resonates with you, ask yourself: What specifically do you anticipate the personal impact would be if there was equity in your organization? What potentially might you gain? What would need to happen in order to achieve a win for all?

Expanding this Way of Being

You may not feel everything related to being Disconcerted applies to you. Maybe there are elements that resonate. Has anything you have read in this chapter evoked a feeling of discomfort? If so, it's possible that the ideas will have threatened some of your core beliefs and values. But ask yourself: Which ones? Is it a deep belief that you are self-made and have achieved your successes through talent and hard work? Is it a belief that the world rewards the best people? Is it an observation that you are being excluded because of your majority characteristics? Or perhaps something else?

Once you've identified your core belief, dial up your attention to the emotions that are triggered when someone suggests this belief might not be fact. Typically, it will be emotions such as defiance, anger, sadness, confusion or even disgust. It can be painful to be challenged in this way.

Let's explore the three main responses to this challenge based on Eric Berne's psychoanalytic theory of transactional analysis.[6] He suggests that there are three 'ego states' from which we can choose to act: parent, adult and child.

In the child state, we revert to a learnt behaviour, based on how we responded to a negative interaction as a child. It's conditioned in us, if you like, that when we fundamentally disagree with someone, we feel a certain way – we experience an associated visceral response – and the subsequent behaviour we demonstrate becomes a predictable pattern. In child state, we are like the proverbial baby throwing its toys out of the pram. For others around us, it might be experienced as hostility, resistance and rebellion.

In the parent state, we react in a way that emulates how our parents, or another voice of authority, responded to us when we didn't agree with them. It's a protective response, holding on to the certainty of what we believe is right and dismissing other perspectives because they don't make sense to us. To others, this can come across as superior, aggressive and harsh.

Both of these are unconscious, automatic responses based on learnt patterns of behaviour. In order to interact from the adult state, we first need to notice what our default response is and, most importantly, we need to want to shift out of it. Motivation is key here. Being in the adult state takes a sophisticated level of maturity as it is all about letting go of what our brains are telling us we should think and feel, and critically analysing the concepts in an open and rational way. I speak about being open with respect to different ideas but also in how you embody openness, which means putting your guard down and being vulnerable to the challenges that you face.

 ### Developing a Receptiveness to Learn

Just as affinity bias suggests, we regularly surround ourselves with people who think like us and, therefore, confirm our beliefs. This is exacerbated via social media these days. The algorithms are so sophisticated that once you start following and liking certain people, your stream fills with more people saying similar things.
If you have elements of a Disconcerted Way of Being, leverage your curiosity and find opportunities for group learning. Whether it's a group coaching circle or a group of leaders attending an inclusive leadership programme, open yourself to conversations where you can hear other people's experiences. In doing so, you may discover that colleagues you have sat next to for years don't necessarily experience the organization as you do. This is a helpful way of building your Receptiveness to Learn about yourself and DEI.

Chapter summary

In this chapter, I discussed how those with a Disconcerted Way of Being tend to push back on DEI as a result of feeling sidelined from the conversation and being made to feel guilty for their overrepresented characteristics, which doesn't seem fair. I explained our fundamental human need to fit in and connect with others and how this fuels our affinity bias – that is, having a preference for people like us. Being aware of this bias often evokes discomfort, because it leads us to question our decision-making as well as whether our successes in life are purely based on talent alone. I unpacked the concept of privilege and how the deep, uncomfortable work is noticing the experiences that are *absent* in our lives but which others encounter on a daily basis.

Challenging the system of inequity is tough, particularly for those who are used to enjoying (whether consciously or not) the power it currently offers them. Disconcerted leaders often have a fear of acknowledging privilege, because if they recognize privilege exists, that forces them to choose to either take action or remain complicit. If DEI work is successful, it will mean change for all, and that prospect brings about uncertainty over what that might look and feel like. Finally, I discussed using the principles of transactional analysis to help you identify your emotions and help navigate the discomfort of DEI in a mature, open and 'adult' way.

Questions of discomfort

If you found that elements of this chapter resonate with your perspective on DEI, you may find it helpful to use the questions below to further facilitate your thinking. This list is available on the Beyond Discomfort website (www.beyond-discomfort.com) as a free downloadable worksheet with space for you to note down your thoughts.

o   What is your tolerance for being wrong? Think of the last time you realized you were acting on a false truth? What did it feel like and how did you respond?

o   Can you think of a time when you have embodied openness? What did you experience in this moment?

o   If you are open to the idea that you may have achieved your success in life partly due to your diversity characteristics, what questions about your identity does this provoke? How does asking these questions of yourself make you feel?

o   How could you remain curious and open to uncovering bias in the workplace despite rarely being able to see its existence or quantify its impact?

o   How could you deepen your understanding by learning about the exclusionary experiences of those with different diversity characteristics to you?

o   If you were to let go of any fear associated with acknowledging your privilege and surrender to the concept that society is biased, where would this lead you?

o   If you were to give yourself agency around the DEI table, what could you offer and what might you gain?

o   If a world that is more inclusive means it places you in a less desirable and more regularly uncomfortable position, in what ways might you still benefit?

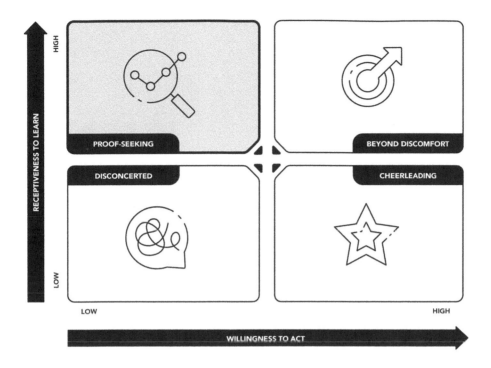

3 Proof-Seeking

We have a natural craving for stability, to know what's going to happen next and so, when we're fearful, it's an easy step to over-control.
                                   —Dr Pippa Grange, psychologist and author[1]

Unlike the Disconcerted Way of Being, leaders who are Proof-Seeking don't necessarily feel threatened and sidelined in the DEI discussion. They want to learn more but have a reluctance to accept, without evidence, what is being described. So, whilst the top left-hand box in the Beyond Discomfort® model represents a high Receptiveness to Learn, Proof-Seeking leaders are also sense-making based on their established truths and what they observe as reality, and when the information doesn't stack up, they are more likely to disregard it, which creates a low Willingness to Act.

As you read this chapter, it's helpful to have your natural leadership tendencies in mind. For example, do you prefer to make decisions once you have all the data? What type of information are you likely to trust or distrust? Who do you trust for information and who do you not trust? Would you rather have a clear path forward before taking action? What is your relationship with uncertainty? If you have taken the Myers-Briggs Type Indicator assessment and have a preference for 'Thinking' (favours quantitative, logic-based, scientific approaches) over 'Feeling' (values emotions and makes decisions on gut instinct), you might relate well to the Proof-Seeking Way of Being.[2]

In this chapter, I share how issues of injustice and inequity are often invisible, which makes analysis and decision-making hard for Proof-Seeking leaders. I explore this through examples of race, gender and sexuality before explaining how the fear of the unknown acts as a barrier to inclusive leadership. I also offer a technique to tap into your inner thoughts and navigate the discomfort.

The archetypal leader

We all know the traditional archetype of a good leader. They're strong, decisive and tend to be the one in control. They also rarely defer to the judgement of others and have confidence that their way is best. Their sense of surety commands respect and creates followers. You've likely seen examples of this stereotypical leader numerous times in your life, whether it's your bosses, teachers or parents, and certainly many political leaders throughout history have demonstrated this type of leadership. There are also examples in film – for example, the characters of Ethan Hunt (in the *Mission: Impossible* films) and James Bond spring to mind. Just to be clear, this vision of strong leadership isn't a bad one, and often these leaders are highly successful in gaining power and are revered by many.

By no means is it just men who hold this belief about successful leadership. The fact that there have been centuries of prominent male leaders means that our very definition of leadership has been based on a masculine framework. So, in a society and organization that rewards and promotes male leadership qualities, it's unsurprising that other genders have adapted to fit the mould.

Let's take a typical organizational scenario where traditional leadership qualities tend to be most apparent. Molly (anonymized) works for a UK-based research company that was going through a lot of strategic change, impacting staff. When I interviewed her in 2023, she expressed her frustration that senior leaders were informing colleagues their roles were changing and making decisions about people's new responsibilities without consulting anyone:

> For me, it's not inclusive behaviour if I'm not part of those decisions or truly being given a voice to express my needs. I should be consulted, because I know what works best in my area of work, what the challenges are and what the needs are.

When I asked Molly why she thought leaders weren't discussing the changes with staff, she said:

> I don't think its intentional. I don't think the leaders realize how important it is to involve everyone, no matter their seniority level, no matter for how long they've been in the organization. Of course I know that leadership is the decision-making machine so to speak. But that decision-making process needs to be taken after you involve everyone who has the knowledge and experience.

Molly's story isn't unique. Often leaders manage organizational restructuring in this secret squirrel way, believing that it's necessary to hold on to all the decision-making power. Granted, there tends to be a lot of political challenges to navigate and information can't always be widely shared across all staff. However, there are a number of pitfalls with this approach. Firstly, it assumes that leaders are fully connected to the day-to-day operations of the organization and have detailed knowledge of what each staff member does in their role. This is neither possible nor advisable if truly acting as a strategic leader. Secondly, the lack of co-creation and collaboration makes staff feel like they are simply a widget in an organizational machine which neither cares about them nor values their contributions. This then leads to feelings of resentment and distrust, reduced commitment to the organization and poor mental health and well-being. It also creates significant vulnerability for the organization, particularly in times of crisis, because it has learnt to solely rely on the knowledge of those at the top, rather than empowering the collective wisdom of everyone who works there. Thirdly, the decisions that are made rarely match the strategic intentions − after all, unless you understand where you're starting, you can't carve out a path to where you want to be. Ultimately, what this creates is a toxic work environment with an 'us versus them' culture in relation to leadership and staff and people continuously signed off on long-term sick. Such an organization has the fragility of an egg balancing on a stick of spaghetti. Maybe you know of organizations that meet this description − you might even have worked in one.

As a leader, it's important to understand the extent to which you find yourself defending your decisions and actions with narratives like: 'It had to be done that way'; 'We just didn't have the time to consult everyone about everything'; 'Staff aren't aware of everything going on in the organization, so there's a risk that we consult them but can't take their ideas forward and they won't understand why. So that would be more detrimental.'

Both pressure and organizational expectations often make it hard for leaders to move away from what is known to them, what has made them successful and continues to work for them. Strong leaders are open to new ideas and welcome opportunities to disrupt their industry. Think of Steve Jobs, Whitney Wolfe Herd and Jack Ma – though with all of their innovations (Apple, Bumble and the Alibaba Group, respectively), there was a clear market need and tangible data that signposted these incredible founders towards a new way of doing things. Of course, there was an element of risk-taking (what good entrepreneur is without that?), but the hook was there.

With inclusive leadership, the hook is there too, but it is often invisible to those in the majority groups, who tend to have the most power. One of the most helpful analogies I have come across was offered by Paolo Gaudiano, Chief Scientist at Aleria (a science-based DEI research organization), when I spoke to him on my podcast:

> When you meet somebody, you don't say 'Hi, I'm Paolo and I'm healthy today.' But if I happen to have a cough, or if my voice is hoarse, or if I had a cast or something, the conversation of my lack of health would come up. So, we don't notice when we're healthy; we notice when we're unhealthy. Similarly, we don't notice when we're being included; we notice when we're excluded.

Those with a Proof-Seeking Way of Being, therefore, are trying to make sense of DEI through their own lens of what is true and real for them. In psychology, this is known as an 'anchoring bias' – that is, the tendency to place more validity on the initial information we have (in this case, our personal experiences) and less on new information (other people's experiences). Therefore, although those who are Proof-Seeking are curious to expand their understanding, they are not necessarily accessing the information they need to do so, which leads to a limited number of answers and a growing number of questions.

'Playing the race card'

I was having dinner with a couple of friends recently and one, a White, female senior leader at a global consulting firm, explained her challenge with managing a Black woman in her team:

She's just not meeting the mark in terms of the quality of her work. I had a conversation with her about it, explaining specifically what needed improving and offering support. But she didn't take it in the way I intended and said it was because she was Black. What am I supposed to do now? I have to manage her and I would do the same if anyone was underperforming, but now I feel really anxious that whatever I say or do will be attributed to her race.

This is a really complex one to unpack, but let's try. Imagine you wake up in the morning and have a giant spot on your nose. There is absolutely no way of covering it – you'll just have to go about your day as usual and hope it goes away quickly. But everywhere you go, people just keep staring – either really obviously or with a not-so-subtle eye movement to your nose before regaining eye contact with you. You're so aware of it and it dominates your thoughts during all your conversations that day. In other words, the spot becomes pertinent to who you are and influences how you interact with the world and how it responds to you.

In a similar way, for people from minority ethnic groups, the colour of their skin is pertinent to who they are, because the world has made it so. We can go back three hundred years to their ancestors and see the horrific treatment of racially marginalized people, seen as objects to be used and abused. Whilst slavery has been abolished, the negative stereotypes associated with Black people – lazy, aggressive, intellectually inferior, unclean (whilst uncomfortable to name, it's important we have a shared reference point) – are deeply etched into society and pervade all aspects of contemporary life. The racially motivated attacks and murders that were across the media in 2020 are evidence of the prejudice that still exists. It can be so deep and hidden that even those who are actively pro diversity and inclusion may not be aware that they are acting on it. Imagine then, walking through the world being acutely aware that there is a part of you that strongly determines how people respond to you, and never being sure when or how overtly it might show up. Not only that, prejudice might be so subtle, such as your line manager being less patient in supporting your development compared to White colleagues, that it can only be felt rather than proven.

When people talk about 'playing the race card', they are suggesting that minority ethnic individuals are using racism to their advantage in order to get sympathy, have special treatment or, in the case described by my friend, get away with not doing a good job. This delegitimizes the experiences of people on the receiving end of racism, denying it as a possible reality.

A leader with a Proof-Seeking Way of Being might read this and understand the points made but still ask the question: 'But *how will we ever know?'* Is it possible that this White, female leader was managing the performance of her Black team member in the same way she would have a White team member? Yes. Is it possible that she was unconsciously acting on stereotypes and biases, which meant she questioned her Black team member's competence quicker than if they had been White? Also, yes.

There are three things that need to happen in order understand what's going on here. Firstly, the White female leader needs to let go of her absolute confidence that she isn't acting on any biases and be willing to explore her beliefs and internal narratives about her Black team member and Black people in general. This is not a typical thing to do and therefore, if done properly, will likely be uncomfortable. Secondly, she needs to show courage and open up an uncomfortable conversation with her Black team member, asking what it is that she has said or done that makes her colleague feel that she is being performance managed because of her race. It's important that this comes from a place of genuine curiosity rather than a defensive 'prove it' mindset. Thirdly, her Black team member needs to feel psychologically safe in order to be able to have this new type of conversation, and feel confident that whatever she shares won't be to her further detriment. You can see why these conversations rarely happen.

The gender pay gap myth

I often hear criticism of the way the gender pay gap is calculated. In essence, organizations can calculate the difference between the mean or median hourly pay by gender. For those driven by data, that doesn't provide a satisfactory measure, because it doesn't compare like for like in terms of what men and women are doing in the organization. Women tend to be in lower-skilled jobs and men tend to be in higher-skilled roles, and so men will be paid more on that basis.

The question is: do women choose to be in lower-paid roles to suit their lifestyle, most likely involving caring responsibilities? Here's where it becomes complex. For sure, there are a number of women who leave the workforce entirely after having children because they decide they want to be present and available. There are also those who sacrifice their careers because of gender expectations about what a 'good' mother should be. When our first daughter was five months old, I won a scholarship to do an Executive MBA at Henley Business School. My excitement was dampened, however, with a series of comments about how brave I was to consider taking it on with such a young baby. One friend asked me if

I was concerned about leaving my daughter once a month, since a lot of research shows how important the presence of a mother is in the first year of a child's life. Yet, one male MBA colleague had a baby mid-way through the course and it seemed that all he got was congratulations. However, just as in Paolo Gaudiano's earlier example relating to health, my MBA friend would never know that the reaction he got was different to mine, because it didn't happen to him.

There are a significant number of professional and highly qualified women who feel that the way their jobs are designed and the expectations in their organizations will not work in their favour when it comes to childcare arrangements. These women end up doing jobs that are below their abilities, and pay grades, in order to remain in work. Some would argue that it is still a choice – that the woman isn't prepared to be as committed to her role as she was before having children. But who determines the culture of the organization and the parameters of success? Industries are often so steeped in patriarchal tradition that it just isn't clear how demanding senior roles could be achieved in any way other than 50 plus hours a week. Why should things change if the current way of working is achieving successful business outcomes? In this sense, it's far easier to assume that it is the woman who has chosen a different career path rather than face the uncomfortable truth that an organization's culture only rewards and promotes people who can dedicate their lives to it.

Using a sophisticated simulation, Paolo Gaudiano and his colleagues at Aleria have been able to quantify how a company culture impacts people with different diverse characteristics. He explained on the *Why Care?* podcast:

> We replicated very simple aspects of individuals' behaviour and how they interact with each other. And then we allowed the computer simulation to play out all of these really complex scenarios – people going to work, having a negative encounter, getting promoted, getting raises, dealing with personal life in the midst of work.

He designed a simulation of a basic company with four layers, from entry level to executive level, with an equal number of men and women at each level. The company grows over time, and when people leave, new people come in and others get promoted to higher levels. In one simulation, he wanted to explore the impact of gender bias in promotions and created the programme so that men were slightly favoured over women.

> Fairly quickly, in… 5 to 10 years, you see a company that becomes exactly what you see in the real world, where the top echelons are dominated by men. And then you get fewer and fewer men as you go down, until eventually at the entry level,

paradoxically, you have more women than men, because the women are stuck there while their male counterparts are getting promoted.

He added:

And what's beautiful is that you can also track the satisfaction when people are not getting promoted, who feel that they should be. And when you do that, you see that the satisfaction of the women plummets and the satisfaction of the men stays very constant. And that reflects very much what you see in the real world, where you find that women tend to have much higher turnover. And often they truncate their careers, or they switch jobs because they're not satisfied, because they see all this unfairness around them.

Now, one could argue that this isn't proof that bias exists, but merely displays what happens when different genders face different circumstances. Is it possible that the common scenario of White men progressing to the top of the organization is purely due to them being better at their jobs, or more committed to work, than any other demographic counterpart? Yes. Is it also likely that an organization designed by men will have processes and systems that favour people like them? Absolutely.

So, what needs to happen? Those in the majority groups who find themselves achieving higher levels of organizational status need to start actively interrogating the system in search of bias. For example, what are the diversity characteristics of those who make promotion decisions? Are behaviours typically displayed by those in the majority rewarded in the organization? What is the organizational attitude towards part-time, flexible and remote workers? Is this consistently applied in all areas of the organization, by every manager? For those with a Proof-Seeking Way of Being, it will be important to search for the evidence, as it's unlikely to be immediately apparent.

'Pretend' sexualities

When I was growing up in the 1980s, homosexuality was taboo. Certain male celebrities – Freddie Mercury is one example – were known to be gay, but so many gay men, and particularly lesbians, remained closeted for fear of how their friends and family would react and what it would mean for their careers, as well as fear of physical harm. Homosexual slurs were common in everyday language and used as insults generally. Over the decades, being lesbian or gay has gradually become more acceptable in certain parts of the world, although we are far from a situation where these groups can feel safe in all domains of life. Even if the idea of homosexuality continued to make some heterosexual people feel uncomfortable, over time most have at least become willing to acknowledge a binary categorization of either heterosexual or homosexual. As humans, we do tend to like simple and easy!

For some heterosexual people, it has been uncomfortable, as well as highly confusing, to *suddenly* be in a world with many sexualities. Of course, it isn't sudden at all – homosexuality has always existed. But in their reality, it feels like that. Just because I work as a DEI professional, that doesn't make me immune to this discomfort or lack of understanding of a community that I don't identify with. In my podcast conversation with Bendita Cynthia Malakia, formerly Chief Diversity & Inclusion Officer at Hogan Lovells, she helped educate me: 'The longest acronym that I've heard for the community is LGBTQQIAP2S, and that stands for lesbian, gay, bisexual, trans, queer, questioning, intersex, asexual, pansexual and two-spirited.'

For heterosexual people, particularly of (but not restricted to) an older generation, these definitions are challenging to say the least. Aside from trying to remember them all, they cut to the very core of many people's beliefs about sexuality and identity.

Bendita illustrated this in our discussion about bisexuality:

> People don't necessarily believe that bisexuality exists. For instance, people think that bisexual individuals are flaky and indecisive. They find their relationships to be a joke. They often characterize it as a passing phase between heterosexuality and homosexuality, rather than as an identity in and of itself. It tends to be overlooked in particular when they are in opposite-sex relationships, because people just decide you're no longer bisexual or a sexual orientation minority. And in those particular cases, oftentimes, the oppression against them is insidious, and it's hidden.

As we expand the labels for different sexualities, there is common pushback from parents (although not from them exclusively) that we are confusing our children with all these options. One of the reasons why we are lacking proof that multiple sexualities aren't simply the latest fad is due to what is known as the 'missing queer generation'. This refers to the young LGBTQ+ people in the 1970s and 1980s. This was a time when violent attacks against homosexual people were not uncommon and discrimination meant poor healthcare provisions, leading to a higher mortality rate. Most notably, the AIDS pandemic caused a high number of premature deaths in gay men. In the US, by 1995, one in 15 gay men had died of AIDS.[3] This has contributed to the current lack of older and senior LGBTQ+ role models in organizations, who potentially would have made it to the C-suite but sadly died before their time.

Once again, it can be argued that there is a lack of clarity and evidence in the domain of sexual orientation. Is it possible that we have socially constructed these alternative identities, and that by creating these other categories, we are confusing people who used to be clear on their sexuality? Maybe. Is it possible that the full range of sexual identities has always existed but weren't allowed to be outwardly displayed? Most definitely.

Sexual orientation is a DEI area where leaders have to dig deep to be willing to explore, because it can go against their values, religious beliefs or the legislation in their country. For those who are Proof-Seeking, it's far easier to deny the existence of other sexual identities than deal with the discomfort of education and learning. It takes a certain amount of curiosity to explore why there aren't any people from the LGBTQ+ community in your organization (or why people might not feel able to disclose their sexual identity). It also requires vulnerability to acknowledge that you did not understand different sexualities but are willing to learn.

 Reverse DEI mentoring

Reverse DEI mentoring programmes pair up junior individuals who have minority diversity characteristics with senior leaders who don't have lived experience of those identities. This can be an incredibly powerful way for people to learn about other communities and demystify some of the things they struggle with. It can also be hugely beneficial to the individuals with diverse identities, as it gives them access to and potential sponsorship from a senior person in the organization.

However, it's important to take care that this is not exploitative. There is a great example from the *Greatest Showman* movie when the hero, P.T. Barnum, sets up a circus of 'freak' performers – such as a bearded lady and a man covered in hair – for people's entertainment. And for minority individuals, whilst they may feel honoured to be noticed and invited to share their experiences, it shouldn't be about seeing them as a curiosity and something to be worked out. Equally, it's important that diverse junior colleagues aren't viewed by leaders as the path to DEI enlightenment. One way to overcome this would be for the leaders to expand their knowledge and understanding through reading, podcasts, events, etc. and come to reverse mentoring conversations with an existing level of understanding. This avoids situations where the person from the marginalized background is doing all the educating.

Fear of the unknown

As a coach, I can easily spot leaders with a Proof-Seeking Way of Being, because I can visibly see the moments of utter confusion on their face as I ask questions that challenge their current observations of the world. I was recently working with a coachee in a global technology company. He was what I call a 'binary thinker'. In other words, he analysed problems to an extreme level of detail, relying on his scrutiny of the data and information to then confidently come to the 'truth'. He believed his views were objective once he had drawn on all possible data sources, but was confused why others weren't as ready to embrace his solutions.

He explained, 'I just don't understand why my colleagues want to continue discussing options. We're wasting time, I've done the analysis and I know I'm right.'

I challenged him by asking 'What could your colleagues be seeing that you're not?'

'Nothing. I've looked at all the data and weighed up all the different scenarios. It's really tiring going over it again and again. I know what we need to do.'

I asked, 'What do you think their needs are in this?'

He paused, puzzled and unable to answer. So, I tried an alternative path: 'How might your confidence in decision-making impact how you are perceived as a leader?'

'I think my colleagues see me as someone who is reliable and consistently thorough, so they can trust that I know what I'm talking about', he replied.

'Yes, I can see how that would be the case. Could there be any downsides to your confidence?', I prompted.

'I can't see any', he answered.

My coachee had so much confidence that he knew right from wrong and could tell truth from fiction, and it was all based on his belief that data holds all the answers. Despite my concerted efforts as a coach, he was unable or unwilling to see that there could be different versions of 'right' or the 'truth' which weren't based on tangible information but on things that he couldn't easily see or measure. If he opened himself up to believing in this possibility, then what would that say about all his past decisions? How could he ever be confident about anything ever again?

Throughout our coaching sessions, I could feel his defence mechanisms shoot up whenever I tried to challenge his Way of Being. It was so deep-rooted in who he was, so fundamental to his world, that no doubt it felt really uncomfortable and frustrating to be asked those questions. It must have felt like I was attacking him somehow. This of course wasn't my intention, but the coaching process relies on the coachee being willing to explore their Way of Being in service of their self-development goals. You have probably deduced that this was not one of my most successful coaching experiences.

Being an inclusive leader, in many ways, sits in juxtaposition to the traditional leadership qualities discussed earlier in the chapter. Strength isn't about clear decisions and always knowing the answers, but about being open-minded and curious about other people's experiences, ideas and thoughts. It is important to acknowledge that this may not be naturally easy for some individuals who have lower natural ability for empathy and find it difficult to understand perspectives and experiences different from their own. However, the difference for those with a Proof-Seeking Way of Being, who have taken pride in being confident in their leadership competency, is that they tend to hold back from doing so out of both defensiveness and fear.

Rose Cartolari, Founder and CEO of RC Consulting, explained on the *Why Care?* podcast: 'Of course, we like certainties. We don't like hearing *"I can be an incredibly talented CEO or manager and still not know this piece."* We don't like holding those two different things together – we like to be competent, because otherwise we're not competent.'

The fear of the unknown stems from trying to imagine what our leadership might look like when we openly acknowledge things that we're not good at and ask others to help bridge the gap. It comes from stepping away from a world of binaries – right and wrong, good and bad, competent and incompetent – and not knowing what being somewhere in-between means. Not just what it means with regards to leadership behaviour, but also how people will perceive you if you start questioning yourself and saying that you might not have the answer. You have to believe that your vulnerability will show strength rather than weakness, which might go against what you have seen and known in leaders before you. Think of the scene in *Indiana Jones and the Last Crusade* when our hero has to bravely step off the cliff and believe that there is an invisible bridge to step onto. Inclusive leadership is a trust exercise like no other. You have to believe that another reality exists without experiencing it yourself.

The only way to discover alternative truths is to be open-minded and curious, actively seeking to spend time with people who are different to you, listening to other perspectives and being willing to realign your own beliefs. It's a tall order. Through discussions with participants in my workshops, I have uncovered various anxieties about this process.

Firstly, leaders tend to be fearful about not being perceived as genuine. One participant questioned: 'What am I supposed to say to the person?… *"I'd really like to know about you, because I don't know anyone who's gay"?'* Other leaders have voiced their uncertainty about what the rules are when entering a conversation with a different diversity group. A participant asked: 'What if I don't agree with that community's beliefs or views? What do I do with that? Do I need to accept everything of this community, and let go of my own beliefs?'

Let's take a moment to examine what's behind this. I sense an anticipated feeling of awkwardness about being with a group of people who have a very different view of the world. Also a feeling of discomfort that comes with not belonging and being a guest. That's a feeling that many people in majority groups are not as familiar with because they are used to having licence to be in a space and to share their opinions freely. I couldn't tell you the number of times I have been asked, sometimes randomly by complete strangers in a shop, 'Where are you from?' This is a common and well-known 'subtle act of exclusion', which is emotionally triggering for me and inevitably leads me to offer a deliberately obtuse response. Behind their request is likely a genuine interest in learning more about my background. But behind their questions also lies the message, 'I can tell you're not from here, so where do you belong?' Despite being UK-born, I have lived my life feeling like a guest, conscious of the British way and aligning as closely as possible to feel like I fit in. It's a skill I have practised. However, it is unlikely this skill would have been exercised as much by those with majority characteristics, which is why the thought of actively entering this space is daunting.

 ### Creating a shadow board

Depending on where you and your senior leadership team are on the DEI journey, you may want to consider establishing a shadow board – this is an initiative adopted by Centrica in 2021.

As Devi Virdi, Group Head of Diversity and Inclusion at Centrica, explained in our discussion on my podcast:

> This is a group of colleagues who come from different parts of our business, and they provide a perspective to our leadership team – they speak truth to power. And every shadow board buddy has an individual in their leadership team that they're married up with. They learn from each other's lived experiences, what is happening in that professional space and what is happening in their own lives. They have regular contact with the leaders, and actually the leaders trust them enough to talk straight to them. That is powerful in itself.

This is such an innovative way for people from majority groups to minimize the fear of attending a community event or networking group whilst, at the same time, giving leaders the experience of hearing alternative views and perspectives. However, in order to set this up for success, it's important that all members of the senior leadership team have high Receptiveness to Learn. If even one or two leaders aren't ready to embrace the learning opportunity from the shadow board members, then the process risks being seen as lip service rather than genuine.

On my podcast, Bendita Cynthia Malakia shared her perspective on how to engage a community different to one's own:

> It doesn't mean that people have to let go of their views. I mean, they wouldn't be values if they were so easily released or swayed. But what it does mean is having

a willingness and openness to suspend your beliefs. If you're in a space with underrepresented people, it's not really for you to impose your views. Depending on the dialogue, you may be able to contribute actively. But it's more for you to respect the space and to engage in learning. You shouldn't be going there with the intent of trying to put your view on others.

Another fear of the unknown that is worth exploring is related to the intangible nature of DEI. Ultimately, leaders are wary because it's impossible to apply fixed rules to inclusive leadership and to know the most inclusive action to take in every situation. What do they need to do to ensure everyone feels that their voice is valued and heard? If exclusion is invisible to those in the majority group, how can they possibly know when they are inadvertently excluding?

The thing is that those who are Proof-Seeking are looking for all the answers before taking action, in the hope that it'll feel more comfortable. There's an element of pragmatism here, articulated beautifully by global DEI leader Sámi Ben-Ali in our podcast discussion:

You can't hold it against someone if they've never had exposure to your lived experience. Why would they necessarily think about it in the same way as me? To really step into that space as a leader, you can't have all the answers – it's impossible. If we were good at everything, we wouldn't have teams. And so, for me, inclusive leadership is showing that vulnerability, showing that I don't have all the answers but I'm willing to find out, I'm willing to ask the questions, I'm willing to step towards that discomfort.

Expanding this Way of Being

If I'm honest, I have some Proof-Seeking in me. In fact, I think part of my training as a psychologist, coach and MBA has deliberately developed my skill for critical thinking and questioning, which makes me want to find evidence and inquire more deeply. It makes me good at my job. But it has also led me to question the validity of other people's lived experiences when hearing them for the first time. In the early 2010s, when working in a London local authority, I was fortunate to have a wonderfully diverse team with many from Black heritage backgrounds. Through conversation, I learnt that as well as Afro hair being a common topic of conversation amongst strangers, those people would often have such curiosity that they would touch my colleagues' hair without permission. I was sceptical – I couldn't imagine someone reaching out to touch a stranger's hair. More significantly, why would they want to? The conversation ended with my inner voice still questioning their stories.

I started to search online on the subject and was blown away by what I learnt. Over the years, I continued to learn by watching TED Talks, including *No. You cannot touch my hair!* by DEI campaigner Mena Fombo,[4] and reading news articles about students who had been sent home from school because their hair didn't adhere to 'school uniform policy'. I realized that race-based hair discrimination genuinely existed!

The privilege I have of working in the DEI space is that I am constantly being offered people's lived experiences. Of course, my sceptical inner voice still exists when I hear a story that doesn't resonate with my reality, but I am now much more practised at hearing it and turning down the volume.

Tuning in to your inner voice is essential as an inclusive leader. On my podcast, Rose Cartolari gave a helpful example in her commentary about patriarchy:

> I hear comments from CEOs and from managing directors who are discussing people's promotions – 'Oh, well, she's not ready.' She's not ready? Really? Is that about her? Or is that about what you think is ready? Or what a male thinks is ready? So, I think we're always caught there. We don't do the work on saying: 'So why don't I think they're ready? What would that mean for me? And do I view women differently than I do men? Do I tend to like this kind of person rather than that person? Why does that person irritate me? Why do I keep making the same decisions?' Really getting into an analysis of myself.

Let's practise an analysis of self. Notice the first comments or thoughts that run through your mind about the person in each of these scenarios:

o   You walk down a busy high street and see a Black man being stopped by the police.

o   As you find your seat on an aeroplane, you realize that some of it is being taken by an overweight man in the seat next to you.

o   One of your young, female colleagues is wearing a low-cut top and very short skirt to a business conference.

o   A single mother in your team who regularly misses deadlines and is late for meetings says she feels overlooked for a development opportunity.

o   Despite coaching and support, your team member still isn't writing in a style that meets expectations.

o   Your colleague sugarcoats the results of a recent staff survey in an endeavour to please her boss.

Be honest, did your inner voice question what the Black man had done? Did it wonder how the overweight man could get into such a state of unhealth? Did it question the professionalism of the young, female colleague? Did it question the capability of your team member? Maybe your inner voice said none of these things, but one thing is certain: it said something. We are constantly talking to ourselves. We are just not observant when it comes to this internal dialogue.

Start paying attention to your inner voice and notice what it's telling you about the people you come across in your daily life. Do this for a while and you'll be able to notice how quick you are at drawing conclusions compared to remaining open to finding out more. For the majority of people, this sort of assessment about what is going on will remain unchecked. To start looking at this more deeply, it's important to first recognize that what we take as fact is purely based on our own lived experiences and that other realities exist that we are as yet unaware of. We can then start identifying our narratives and patterns and ultimately go on a journey to open ourselves up to new possibilities by *catching* our thoughts, *challenging* our thinking and *changing* our stories. This is a useful cognitive behavioural therapy technique which I find leaders can easily implement as a way of positively reframing their thoughts.

Let's use these techniques to look at the first two scenarios in more detail.

Scenario 1: You walk down a busy high street and see a Black man being stopped by the police.

Inner voice: I wonder what he did?

My assessment is based on: Police only stop people for good reason.

Questions: Perhaps that might not apply to everyone? What if there is bias in the system which leads to Black people being stopped more often than other racial groups exhibiting the same types of behaviour? How could I find out more about this?

Scenario 2: As you find your seat on an aeroplane, you realize that some of it is being taken by an overweight man in the seat next to you.

Inner voice: How did he let himself get to such an unhealthy state?

My assessment is based on: We're all in control of how we treat our bodies.

Questions: What diseases are associated with obesity? What psychological conditions are connected to weight gain? How might the way people treat overweight individuals impact their condition?

Try using this technique with the remaining four scenarios. How do the questions help challenge your internal dialogue and assessment? If you are Proof-Seeking like a scientist or mathematician in search of a clear answer, you might find this process frustrating and unsatisfying. Inclusive leadership is not a science. Humans are not rational beings; we are led by emotions and values. So, this practice of holding your own world view with lightness and inviting alternative possibilities into your reality is key. Notice the discomfort of unlearning your truth as fact and relearning multiple truths. This is deep work and it isn't easy, but when you open yourself up to seeing the world through a different lens, it inevitably leads to different behaviour and outcomes.

 Developing a Willingness to Act

It's fair to say that you don't know what you don't know. Therefore, if you or other leaders have a Proof-Seeking Way of Being, you may not actively start challenging your assessments without any reason. I have found a number of methods can help facilitate this process:

o *The power of the group* – inviting discussion between colleagues so they can share personal stories and learn something about each other that they never knew before can be incredibly impactful in dialling up curiosity and driving motivation to take action.

o *Experiential learning* – simulation exercises, role plays, case studies and forum theatre (a role play-style set-up where participants practise new behaviours in a safe space) are a few ways to learn by doing. The practical process is useful for transferring learning to real life, and plenary debrief sessions are equally as valuable. For example, when inclusive behaviours are demonstrated in the group, reflect on what you saw and how it made you feel. You can then better understand what the person did and the impact it had.

o *Coaching practice* – it's important to support your capacity to ask more questions (both inner inquiry and expanding your understanding of others). Building practical coaching skills into your development is incredibly valuable. You will likely find it a helpful tool to learn from others and provoke deeper thought into ideas that you may never have considered before.

Chapter summary

In this chapter, I challenged the traditional and embedded beliefs of what leaders should be, inviting Proof-Seeking leaders to dig deeper to find the hook for inclusive leadership, which isn't always immediately obvious. Curiosity is fundamental here, as is expanding our understanding of reality, which is based on our own experiences, and being open to seeing alternative truths. This can be deeply uncomfortable, because it calls into question the foundations of the ground we stand on as leaders.

I illustrated the complexity of DEI and the existence of multiple possibilities by drawing on examples of race, the gender pay gap and bisexuality. I invite you, as a leader, to hold your perspectives with lightness and, as much as possible, try to avoid the common pitfall of binary thinking. Often those with a Proof-Seeking Way of Being feel discomfort with the nuances of DEI and the lack of clear data that points to a 'right' answer. Being able to let go of a binary approach and acknowledge the existence of multiple truths is key to inclusive leadership. Using the cognitive behavioural technique of catch, challenge, change can help you tune in to your inner dialogue and support you in remaining open and curious.

Questions of discomfort

If you feel aligned with some of the Proof-Seeking views, you may find it helpful to use the questions below to further facilitate your thinking. Use the free downloadable worksheet on the Beyond Discomfort website (www.beyond-discomfort.com) to note down your thoughts.

o   What is your tolerance for not having a clear answer? What do you typically experience in your body when you face uncertainty? How is noticing this useful with regards to DEI?

o   What DEI concepts and conversations raise more questions than answers for you? What is it specifically about what you are hearing that doesn't make sense for you?

o   If you were to recognize your assessments related to these issues and park them for a moment, what do you become curious about? What might be the alternative truths that you aren't yet aware of?

o   Where could you look for more information that could help open up your thinking and awareness of other possibilities?

o   If you were open to the possibility that not all truths have tangible evidence, how might this influence your decision-making approach?

o   How can you create an environment where people know you are open to other possibilities and feel safe to share?

o   In service of learning multiple truths, how might you display mature vulnerability with your colleagues? What discomfort do you feel about leading in this way?

o   When was the last time you felt like you were a guest in a space where you had less legitimacy to voice your opinions? Where might you find ways to practise the discomfort that such an environment might hold?

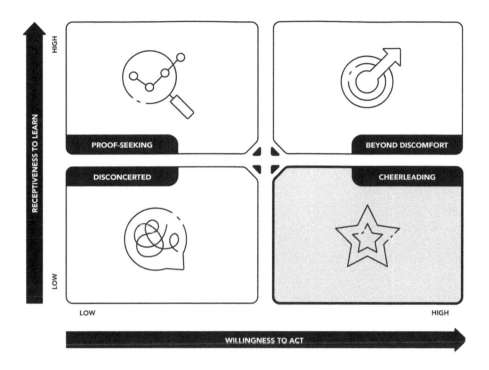

4 Cheerleading

> My mind flips between a belief that I am as good as they come and a belief that I am no good at all. In the end, the belief that I am a good person always wins.
>
> —Dolly Chugh, psychologist and author[1]

In the last chapter, I touched on the binary bias that often filters our lens of the world. We see things in a much more simplistic way than exists in reality. This binary bias is ultimately what forms the basis of the Cheerleading Way of Being. As humans, we have such a deep desire to see ourselves as good people and good leaders, because if we aren't good, then that means we're bad, and that just isn't the case. So, whilst the bottom right-hand box represents a high Willingness to Act, when Cheerleading, leaders demonstrate confidence that they already practise inclusion. Therefore, as they feel they already know all there is to know about inclusive leadership, this creates a low Receptiveness to Learn. As you read this chapter, notice your desire to find evidence of how inclusive you are. For example, do you find yourself remembering how positive diverse team members were about working for you? Are you reflecting on the culturally diverse holidays you've been on and how you embraced different traditions and food? How open are you to being a reasonably good leader – not bad but not perfect either?

In this chapter, I discuss why seeing people's differences often doesn't make sense, but why it is necessary in order to truly lead inclusively. I offer examples of invisible inequities when it comes to race, socio-economic status, neurodiversity, accent and language, and fathering. I go on to explain the discomfort experienced by those who are Cheerleading, which is generated from a fear of complexity, and I offer some advice on how to develop grit and a growth mindset.

This doesn't make sense

When facilitating our inclusive leadership programme, I often hear:

> But if we're trying to create inclusion where everyone feels like they belong, it doesn't make sense to then highlight people's differences and put them into boxes based on their diversity characteristics. People are more than these labels we place on them. I thought that was the whole point of what we were trying to avoid?

It's a fair challenge and it also highlights one of the most common areas of confusion for people with a Cheerleading Way of Being. They have a fundamental belief that being inclusive means treating everyone the same, with fairness and respect.

What I hear in this challenge is confusion over what DEI stands for and what inclusive leaders have to do. For example, in order for people to feel like they fit in, we have to see them as different. Really? I also hear concern over the disregard for consistency in approach. As leaders, in order to avoid any dispute raised against you, the general principle is to treat everyone the same so as to avoid being pulled up for favouritism.

When I married my husband, I joined a White, middle-class and incredibly welcoming family. For any of you who have a cross-cultural partnership, you'll recognize that it comes with certain challenges. These challenges are no one's fault; they simply exist. My husband's family engage in a different type of conversation to my family, find things funny that are baffling to me and place emphasis on different values to the ones my family give importance to. I recognize that some blending and compromising on family traditions is almost always necessary when two families come together, in order to make the new family unit work. However, I also believe this is heightened when cultural differences come into play. When sitting at the dinner table, going for a family walk or going on holiday, I am constantly aware of being the only racial minority in the group. I stand out when I am with my husband's side of our family and it is obvious that I don't innately belong.

Now, you would absolutely be right in challenging that the same could be said for my husband when he is with my side of the family. However, to see the difference in our two situations, you must be willing to explore history in depth. What is the value that has been placed on Whiteness compared to any shade of brown? Even in counties where the majority of people have brown skin, there is generally a preference for being fairer.[2] Women, in particular, who are of a darker skin tone often get bullied, are given nicknames and find it hard to marry due to being seen as less attractive. This dates back to a sign of wealth, as those labouring in the fields all day would have had darker skin due to sun exposure. It also points to a deeply held belief that 'White is best'.

Notice what feeling this evokes in you when you read those words: 'White is best'. If it is something you haven't noticed before, are you open to exploring it?

Colourism (the preference for lighter shades of brown skin) and racism are so deeply embedded in symbols and the language around us that we typically don't notice them.[3] For example, white symbolizes peace and purity, whilst black symbolizes death and evil. In 2016, Nadya Powell, Founder of Utopia, together with casting director Selma Nicholls, launched the Christmas so White campaign to counter the 'Whitewashing' of images in the media, focusing on the absence of images of minority ethnic families enjoying Christmas. The underlying message is that a perfect Christmas is a White Christmas. Whilst in recent years we have seen the emergence of Black characters in comic books, there is still a dominance of White superheroes, and when a superhero gets taken over by evil, there is a tendency for their suit to be darker – think Spider-Man and Venom. When Harry Potter and the Cursed Child first came to London's West End, there was absolute uproar because Black actress Noma Dumezweni was cast as Hermione Granger. This went against what many people believed about Hermione's character – not just that she should have White skin, but potentially also what this represented about the character's virtuousness.

These messages are all around us, and they are picked up and absorbed from a very young age. In one of my workshops, a participant shared: 'My nephew asked for his fourth birthday wish if he could be White.' We don't have to look back to times of slavery to see evidence of 'White is best'; it's right here in our current-day life. So, you see, when I'm with my husband's side of the family, I am carrying all of that invisible trauma, past and present, with me. My husband, on the other hand, has an unconscious assuredness of status that has forever been present and so is equally invisible to him. This is nothing for him or his family to feel guilty about, as they can't control what happened in the past or the pervasive symbols and images in the world around us that reinforce racism. However, there are several things that need to happen in order to make a difference: firstly, acceptance that, on the whole, the world carries a 'White is best' mentality and this influences all that people are, see and believe; and, secondly, taking this power with the responsibility it invokes by bringing a sensitive curiosity to what the invisible trauma is and the consequences of it – that is, how does the historical lower status of having brown skin affect my experience of being in the family?

Errol Amerasekera, Director at Bluestone Edge, calls this trauma 'ghosts in the walls'. In my interview with him in 2023, he said: 'These are historical narratives that no one is talking about... it's not your personal trauma; it's the environment where the collective narrative is playing out.' He went on to explain:

> With slavery, there is genuine trauma there – intergenerational ancestral trauma. But then you put people of Black heritage in an organization where that White-centric narrative is prevalent and then they go: 'Oh, why do I feel insecure when I go to work?' How we experience our capability, our self-esteem or our belonging changes because of the environment created by that unconscious narrative, which is deeply but subtly embedded in the culture.

People with underrepresented characteristics are always carrying ghosts with them, and this plays out in how they interact with the world and vice versa. Bonnie St. John, CEO of Blue Circle Leadership Institute, provided an illustration in our podcast discussion:

> There was a woman of Indian descent who was a member of a country club. And she ran into a senior leader from her company, and he looked at her and he asked, 'When did you become a nanny?', because she was at the country club with children who were very light-skinned. And he looked at her and he saw a nanny – he did not see a professional woman who was a member of the club with her own children.

The baby boomer generation, in particular, were brought up not to talk about race or sexuality. The significance of labelling someone means that you have noticed their difference and therefore must be racist, sexist, homophobic or any other word associated with people who are prejudiced. Of course, whilst this school of thought is more prevalent in the older generation, by no means are they the only ones who state with confidence that they don't see colour or gender or difference of any kind. For those leaders who are Cheerleading, it means they don't hold biases and are as inclusive as it gets. It's important to note that these beliefs are coming from a well-intentioned place. They have a desire to be inclusive. But just as the UK's delay in entering the initial Covid-19 lockdown was intended to create herd immunity, sometimes the intention doesn't lead to the desired outcome.

When I spoke to Pat Phelan, Chief Customer Officer at GoCardless, on my podcast, he explained his journey to realizing this:

> For a long time I would be the first person in the world to say (and it just embarrasses me to say it), 'I do not see colour', 'I do not see gender.' Looking at it now and having researched it, it is the most clichéd, most inaccurate thing someone in my position could ever say. I understand now why that is absolutely counterproductive, because it's not about not seeing it. You have to understand the different paths that people take and the different obstacles that were in front of people in order to be able to engage with folks in a different way.

Invisible inequities

'Equality' and 'equity' are words I often hear used interchangeably. It's only through self-education that leaders recognize and understand the important distinction between the two. Equality is what whose who are Cheerleading believe represents fairness, because it means treating everyone exactly the same, with respect and a consistency of practice across team members. From a human resources (HR) perspective, it's certainly one of the best ways to avoid being taken to an employee tribunal. No leader can be criticized for favouritism if they adhere to equality.

Equity, on the other hand, is about treating people based on their individual needs and in consideration of the unique challenges or barriers that they face because of their diversity characteristics. I often use the analogy of a transport underground system to illustrate this point. Most underground stations have an escalator for people to get down to platform level. Everyone has access to this escalator, so there is equality. However, there are certain people who aren't able to use the escalator because of their specific needs – for example, if they have mobility issues or if they have a pushchair. So if we install a lift, this creates equity, because we have acknowledged that the initial solution wasn't fair for all.

Typically, installing a lift isn't contentious. After all, it's clear that some people can't use an escalator, so the need for equity is obvious. However, workplace inequity is often invisible. It is hidden in the depths of the organization's structures, processes and culture, and it is the result of the power afforded to those who designed the system. An example would be job descriptions that require a certain level of qualification not actually necessary to be successful in the role, which then limit opportunities for people from lower socio-economic backgrounds. I'm not necessarily talking about power in the hierarchical sense, although typically those people for whom the system is designed often encounter fewer barriers to the top. Power also comes from having status throughout history because of diversity characteristics that are in the majority and viewed as 'better'. In most cases, these characteristics are White, male, heterosexual, cisgender, neurotypical, with no physical disabilities.

If you identify with most or all of these characteristics, notice your emotional response to reading this list. It can feel uncomfortable to acknowledge that you identify with a group or groups of individuals who have dominated others in the past and that the historical consequences continue to play out in everyday life. You may look at members of your team and at people across your organization and see plenty of diversity, which is an indication that we have come a long way in creating equal opportunity, even in the last decade. In our 2021 research, *Putting Privilege in Its Place*, one participant explained:

> In my team I've got a variety of different people – some men, some women, different age groups, younger and older, different ethnic backgrounds, two other ladies and they're both Asian, my manager is Black and her manager is Black… but there are White people as well. So, I think there is a good mix.[4]

I agree with the view that we have indeed made significant progress over the past few decades, but seeing diversity across the organization doesn't automatically mean that there is equity and inclusion or that people feel like they belong. Those who are Cheerleading tend to assume that there is diversity in their team and in leadership positions because everyone has been treated the same – that is, their differences have not been acknowledged. But what if they achieved this *despite* being treated the same?

A great example of the measures that can be taken to address inequity is the work of charity Sponsors for Educational Opportunity (SEO), which was founded in 1963 to support young people from under-resourced New York high schools to get into university.[5] They soon realized that whilst the young people were successful in achieving degrees, they weren't obtaining elite roles within major companies. Why? Probably because of their lack of knowledge about where to look for such jobs, lack of experience in completing job applications or not knowing what to say at interviews, and lack of belief that these companies want people 'like them'. SEO expanded their programme to bridge this gap by preparing young people for corporate recruitment and building their confidence. Simultaneously, they reached out to corporates, encouraging them to engage more talented young people from underrepresented backgrounds. SEO offer a positive action programme (discussed in Chapter 2) pursuing fairness by recognizing the inequity at the very grassroots of our society that affects underserved groups, and providing hands-on, high-impact coaching and training. Without this support, the talented young people they support would be unlikely to connect with life-changing opportunities to fulfil their potential.

This was nicely illustrated in my podcast discussion with Sheri Crosby Wheeler, previously Vice President of Global Diversity, Equity & Inclusion at the Fossil Group – a woman of Black heritage who grew up in El Paso, Texas. She described her personal desire to leave Texas as a young girl and meet professionals who looked like her. However, she also described the limitations that adult mentors placed on her because of her background: 'They told me: "Don't leave, you can go to school here." And I replied: "I've been here all this time; I want to leave." I think counsellors should say "Yes, you can do it. Go out there – fly. I believe in you" instead of saying "Nah, play it safe."'

So, we can see how Sheri's personality and drive to pursue more than what people in her town were expecting of her impacted her interactions and experience. We can also imagine how another young Black person with less independent thought and tenacity might have made a different choice. However, if you have only ever experienced encouragement to reach your dreams and have always been uplifted by seeing role models who look like you, how would you ever know that other people experience anything different? This inequity is invisible, yet it has a huge impact on life outcomes. Through their genuine desire to learn about other people's personal experiences, those with a Cheerleading Way of Being can start to uncover the subtleties of how to adapt their leadership approach.

Has potential, lacks focus

The thing about neurodiversity is that it is often invisible to others and unidentified, and it can even leave the individual themselves wondering why they aren't able to function like everyone else. In a special episode of *Why Care?*, my cousin, Elvin Nagamootoo, shared his experience of growing up with unidentified neurodiversity in South East London in the 1980s:

> I struggled with attention, focusing on things... and I think once you have one of those labels applied to you, they tend to stick. If you looked at any of my school reports, they would pretty much say exactly the same thing – 'Nice child, very disruptive, somewhat playful, could do better' is pretty much the kind of consistent things you pull out of them.

He went on to explain:

> It has a big ripple impact when you have those labels applied early on, because you start to fulfil those prophecies. You box yourself into those places and go: 'Well, actually, no, I can only do this.'

Let's unpack what's going on here. The labels Elvin experienced likely came from neurotypical people who observed his behaviour as different and not compliant with the norm. We can see once again that the benchmark is based on the majority group – in this case, neurotypical people. On my podcast, neurodiversity and mental health advocate Sean Betts summarized the consequences of this:

> The world is set up for neurotypical people. And when someone who is neurodiverse tries to fit into that neurotypical world, that can create a lot of stresses and strains on them mentally, that then manifests in broader mental health issues. And that's not to say that everyone who is neurodiverse has a mental health challenge as well. But there is a very strong correlation between the two.

In other words, anxiety and other mental health problems are often the result of the neurodivergent individual trying to adapt to surroundings that are made for neurotypical people.

People with attention deficit hyperactivity disorder (ADHD), which is more commonly associated in boys and men, have difficulties paying attention and organizing, have overactive thinking and act impulsively. It equally has incredibly positive attributes, including having hyperfocus on certain tasks, being good at idea generation and being highly empathetic and personable, but these are often overlooked because everyone is focused on what the person lacks.

We are now starting to realize that there is a lost generation of women with ADHD who have not been diagnosed, arguably due to inequity brought about by male-centric medical research. The impact on unidentified ADHD in women is significant. They have been navigating workplaces with neurotypical managers and established neurotypical ways of working and performance expectations without understanding why it was a challenge for them. In my interview in 2023 with Lesley (anonymized), a 45-year-old woman who recently discovered her ADHD, she shared:

> I always felt I was having to prove myself. But it always came back to these regular tasks that needed to be done. I'd get bored easily, but then I get really drawn into spreadsheets and I'd be avoiding managing a task or, you know, the more ambiguous stuff… That would then build up and I'd then have to answer why I wasn't delivering. And then I'd get stressed and I'd get upset, and I'd stay late in work. I'd be coming in on weekends.

Let's look at the manager's perspective for a moment. You have someone on your team who is underperforming, so you wrap some additional support around them. For example, you set up more regular one-to-one meetings, you encourage them to let you know if they are stuck or aren't able to fulfil a task, you suggest they write lists and systematically go through them in priority order. You can see they are trying, but you can't understand why they aren't able to produce the work you need them to. You deduce it must be a capability issue and so performance manage them out of your team, and maybe even the organization. This sadly leaves the neurodivergent individual with confirmation of their ineptness and inability to do anything properly.

If you are a neurotypical leader, the inequities for neurodiverse colleagues are invisible unless you really examine deeply. What if the way meetings are organized aren't conducive to neurodivergent people engaging in conversation and sharing their views? Perhaps the way roles are designed are for people with strong and consistent executive functioning (that is, ability to plan, focus and multi-task), which many neurodiverse people struggle with? Maybe the way goals are set and performance is measured is skewed in favour of neurotypical people? What if the way the team socializes restricts the participation of neurodivergent colleagues? This is a process of peeling away every aspect of processes, systems and culture to see things through a neurodiverse lens, which may require bespoke changes depending on the specific characteristics of the team member. It's undoubtably a lot of work, but it's clear that by Cheerleading and regarding fairness as treating everyone the same, it's not possible for neurodivergent people to thrive.

Bridging the gap in neurodiversity

We all still have so much to learn about working with people who have neurological differences. Each condition presents differently in each individual. One person's autism might be demonstrated through less eye contact, more direct communication and repetitive behaviours. Another person might show difficulties in their social interactions, leading to misinterpretation and miscommunication. As always, bridging the education gap is critical to developing understanding and empathy. This can be in the form of panel events where neurodivergent staff share their stories, or it might involve bringing in external speakers who can raise awareness and provoke ongoing discussion. Or it might involve signposting people to neurodivergent influencers and authors, such as Professor Amanda Kirby and Fern Brady.

Often the way that jobs and organizational processes are designed can be restrictive for people who are neurodivergent – for example, rigid work schedules or the communication culture in the organization can cause difficulties. The work environment itself can cause issues – for example, bright office lights or loud noise from communal areas can be distracting. Rather than guessing about these aspects, ask neurodivergent staff to offer feedback and ideas through a survey (which can be anonymous if they prefer), or you could run creativity sessions to design for neurodivergence. These are great ways to create psychological safety for neurodivergent individuals, and you can offer support if they choose to self-identify. Ideally, make sure you have an executive sponsor who is actively engaged in the work and, importantly, can influence budget spend.

I don't understand you

Have you ever been frustrated because you've called a customer support line and you just can't understand the accent of the person you're speaking with? Have you ever felt yourself switching off when someone with a broad or thick accent is speaking because it is tiring to follow what they are saying? As a coach, I have worked with clients with strong African and Indian accents and, despite my training in active listening, have found my mind wandering because making sense of what they are telling me is an effort. It's easily done, but what are the consequences for those individuals whose accent or language doesn't comply with the way most people speak in your organization?

Accent bias is prevalent in every country. For example, there may be a north–south divide or a town versus countryside distinction when it comes to accents. This isn't just about how people speak in different areas or the way they use language; it can lead to assumptions about a person's social class, their level of education and their intelligence. I know that I have privilege with my accent. It is a regionally neutral accent used by many middle-class speakers in England. Despite growing up in a low socio-economic household, my parents knew the importance of speaking 'properly' for how my brother and I were perceived by the world around us, so this was continuously picked up on and at the slightest hint of dropping a 't', we were corrected. I have learnt to leverage this privilege in the hope that it helps to counter any biases against me that might be present due to my ethnicity, petite stature and gender. Now imagine reading this last paragraph with the cockney accent of working-class London, a Birmingham accent, a Nigerian accent, an Indian accent, a Chinese accent, a Texan accent and so on. What changes for you in how much weight you place on my words and how much credibility I have as the author?

I'm reminded of a story shared by Michelle Obama in *Belonging*. She describes herself as a young child, chatting to some girls around her age: 'At one point, one of the girls, a second, third or fourth cousin of mine, gave me a sideways look and said, just a touch hotly, "How come you talk like a White girl?" The question was pointed, meant as an insult or at least challenge.'[6] Michelle's difference was unlikely to be purely in her accent and diction alone; it would have also been what she chose to say and how she said it, and in the subtleties of what she chose not to say. The exclusion she experienced was a result of not meeting the linguistic expectations of the group she was with.

When I interviewed Veronika Koller, Professor of Discourse Studies at Lancaster University, in 2023, she explained more about the subtleties of linguistic inequity:

> *People will handle things like silences or interruptions very differently, and that crosses over into intercultural communication. I had a Japanese student who, whenever I asked her a question, would take quite a long pause (from my perception) before she answered. This could be misunderstood as she hasn't understood what I said, but which for her, was actually a politeness marker to show that my question deserved due consideration.*

This is a great example of how we benchmark language etiquette based on how we use language ourselves and the norm in the culture we grew up in. So you can see how an organization which has been founded by a group of White, upper- or middle-class individuals, or which continues to be dominated by those with majority DEI characteristics, might favour people who speak and write in the way they deem to be appropriate. As an example, if you work in government, this might be familiar to you, as there is a certain style and language that ministers want in written reports, and anything that that doesn't meet that standard isn't read. So, if you are responsible for dealing with ministers, you will inevitably be looking for a certain skill set in your team, which will likely mirror the demographics of the ministers so that the development gap is minimized. You can see, then, how a recruitment bias might creep in.

In this example, the use of language is related to class and the invisible inequity is related to social mobility – a 'class ceiling'. In organizations, the standard way of speaking typically correlates with status. So if you are from a lower-class background, your language will be frowned upon and maybe even made fun of, which will affect your self-confidence, self-efficacy and ability to fulfil your potential. Veronika Koller expanded on this in the interview:

> If you work in a corporate culture where whenever you open your mouth, somebody cracks a joke, then you just won't speak anymore. You try to become not invisible, but inaudible. And, of course, that has an obvious impact on your career progression. So, I think it needs to be understood that this is exclusionary, discriminatory, just as a comment on somebody's skin tone would be.

It's also worth stating that sometimes it may not be about overtly undermining those from a lower class, but subtly favouring those from the higher classes, which is much harder to identify and challenge.

From the moment we speak, we involuntarily share certain aspects of our identity, which is constantly being interpreted (and often misinterpreted) by those around us. Those who are Cheerleading try to ignore this difference in an attempt to be fair, but this minimizes people's experiences of constant false assumptions about their intellect, social class and whether they will fit in a team. It may be that, as a leader, you would prefer to get to know someone and refrain from making any assumptions about what their accent or use of language says about them. That would be ideal, but how realistic is it given the complexity of language socialization in an organization? Those with a Cheerleading Way of Being would benefit from being curious about how people's way of speaking impacts them having a voice around the table. What might someone using 'non-conforming' language need to feel psychologically safe to speak?

Communication, by definition, involves at least two people, and so it is important for leaders to recognize their personal responsibility for creating an effective interaction. Firstly, being able to spot your biases when it comes to language and accent is key. Notice what happens within yourself when you are struggling to understand someone – do you switch off, feel frustrated, start speaking slowly or raising your voice, for example? To navigate this auto-response, it may help you to consider each interaction as being in service of the person who is communicating with you. What do they need that will allow them to communicate at their best, and how might you offer this? What might be helpful to share with them in terms of your needs?

The fatherhood forfeit

The year 2014 was significant for me. I became a mum for the first time that January, and I started my Executive MBA that October, which was just as I would have been heading back to work from maternity leave. My husband had already decided to take eight weeks shared parental leave, which had come with its own concerns for his career. No one in his company had yet made use of this government policy, so my husband had to wait whilst the HR department created a form for him to complete. He wanted to take longer off work, but he didn't think his company would adjust his performance metrics and so essentially felt pressure to deliver what he usually would in 12 months, despite taking two months out, to avoid a reduced end-of-year bonus.

My MBA took me away from home one long weekend each month and also on trips to South Africa and China. I knew I wouldn't have been able to do this without my husband's strong desire to be an active and equal parent. However, no matter a man's desire, when moving away from what society perceives his role to be – that is, the provider and breadwinner – he faces a penalty. On my podcast, Yash Puri, Founder of blog and networking site Papa Penguin, described his experience when he announced he was taking three months shared parental leave:

> There's an unconscious bias – a woman gets pregnant and they get it, right, full-time mum looking after the child. If a father says anything above and beyond 'I'm going to be off for two weeks and back in the office again', people say, 'You're going on a long leave; you're going to have great fun – play a bit of golf, skiing, go to the pub.' And that's the perception.

It was clear to me that neither my husband's nor Yash's experiences were unique, so I focused my MBA research on understanding the bias within the organizational system that created inequity in male caring. In one focus group, a father shared his experience:

> My two-year-old son was taken to hospital and I asked my line manager if I could leave the office to go and be with him. She asked me where my wife was. Even when I explained that my wife was already at the hospital but that I wanted to be there too, my line manager still didn't understand why it was necessary.

This speaks to the unsaid rule in organizations and society – women are carers and men are providers. So, in the example here, as this man's wife was already fulfilling the caring role, the line manager couldn't comprehend why this man didn't want to fulfil his role as a provider.

In Season 1 of Why Care?, I spoke to Dr Laura Radcliffe, Reader at the University of Liverpool, who shared:

> It's not beneficial for men to be taken out of that equation of being a carer. It's human nature to want to care and build relationships with your children. The number of times you hear men at the end of their careers saying the biggest regret is that they missed a lot of time with their children growing up.

Despite a deep desire by many fathers to be active in their caring role, the pressure to conform to workplace expectations of being fully committed to their job (including long, unpredictable hours and travel away from home) is the main factor restricting their ability to do so.

As is the case when anyone goes against workplace norms, fathers who work flexibly or reduce their hours because of childcare needs often pay a price. Dr Jasmine Kelland, author of Caregiving Fathers in the Workplace, explains the findings of her research: 'caregiving fathers are identified as encountering a set of forfeits that are twofold. Fathers face a forfeit of being less likely to obtain a role conducive to active caregiving and forfeit a positive workplace experience if they do obtain such a role'.[7] She offers examples of the social mistreatment of men in the workplace when they lean in to their caring responsibilities, including negative judgements, mockery and being viewed with suspicion. Of course, women are more than familiar with their careers being deliberately stalled as a result of their caring duties, but men face a different type of penalty for working flexibly, because it is less acceptable for them than it is for women.

It seems that just as career women pay significant penalties in the workplace when they become mothers, men are also in a no-win situation when they lean in to their caring roles. This workplace inequity for men is often overlooked because we look at the top echelons of most organizations and see that it's mostly men with the power. What we don't ask those men about (and they often are unlikely to offer) is what they have sacrificed to be there. Those who are Cheerleading might treat a caregiving man in the same way as a non-caregiving man or a caregiving woman, but in doing so, they fail to see the unique stigma, barriers and judgements he faces in his daily working life. In other words, it minimizes the 'ghosts in the walls' that he carries.

Reflect, for a moment, on your personal experience of male caring – this might be personally, through your partner or your own father figure as a child. How does this influence your views about working fathers and how you respond to them as a leader? For example, how much time do you generally spend with a new father following paternity leave? It isn't uncommon for fathers to be expected to pick up their work as if they had just been away on holiday. Yet creating space to learn about their unique experience of this important life event is invaluable, and, equally, finding out more about what they need from you and the organization is crucial both upon their return to work and on an ongoing basis as they navigate the road of parenthood. What support exists in your organization for new fathers?

Fear of complexity

When I talk to leaders who are Cheerleading and explain some of what I've discussed in this chapter so far, they often look at me as if I've asked them to pull a rabbit out of a hat. They play back the message in their own words: 'So what you're saying is that in order to lead inclusively, I have to treat people differently based on something that can't be measured or seen?!' In short, yes, that is what I'm asking. However, the inequities are only invisible because we haven't programmed our brains to look for them and we haven't created a safe space in our teams or organizations to open up the conversation.

This of course isn't a quick win and it takes effort (a lot of it). Have you ever watched a movie where there are so many characters, plotlines and twists that you are just completely and utterly lost? You turn to the person sitting next to you on the sofa in the hope that they can either enlighten you or are just as confused as you are and open to the idea of watching something else entirely. Sometimes the directors of these movies have deliberately made an artistic choice to make the plot convoluted, the intention being that viewers will draw their own meanings. But, let's face it, sometimes we just want an easy watch – show me who the protagonist is, let me get absorbed in their bad twist of fate and watch them overcome their archnemesis, and allow me to be thrilled by their victory. The allure of this simplicity is what makes romantic comedies so successful.

And there it is — our desperate desire for inclusive leadership to be easy, more like *When Harry Met Sally* than *The Matrix*!

Life is already hugely complex and challenging. If, by Cheerleading, we can keep it simple and treat everyone in exactly the same way, that would limit our chance of error. However, the reality is that this approach leaves those who are Cheerleading more open to error. One participant in a workshop in 2022 offered a helpful example: 'Not seeing colour is like saying to someone in a wheelchair: "I don't *see wheels*". But that means you haven't considered how they move around in the world, the challenges they face and how it's historically been used against them.'

The complexity of what being an inclusive leader requires can be hugely overwhelming. Imagine you have a team of five people. Each person has their own intersectional diversity characteristics, cultural background, personality and personal lived experiences that they carry with them. They don't always share these, but they influence how each person interacts with the world. They are working within an organizational system that has an insurmountable number of processes, policies, routines and cultural norms, often intangible, which respond differently to each team member. In addition to this, there are societal expectations that influence how each person in your team sees the other team members, and forms the basis for their relationships and impact the psychological safety within the team environment. All of these things form what is akin to a tightly and irregularly woven ball of wool, which, if you tug at it, may or may not give you the information you need in order to lead inclusively.

Even with your good intentions of inquiring more deeply about each person's experiences, there is still the complexity of language to navigate. In another workshop in 2022, two participants had the following discussion:

'The conversations happen so fast due to the internet – the linguistics change very quickly – I think it's complicated. You need to keep up with this language so you are aware and don't offend.'

'I agree. I can't get my head around all the letters of LGB… whatever. I think it's incredibly complicated and that's where I have reservations about saying anything.'

'Yes, it's tricky that right and wrong aren't clear. If you make a mistake in public, you are cancelled by the masses.'

Underlying this conversation is fear, born out of this complexity, of saying the wrong thing, but also fear of the consequences of not effectively navigating the complexity. Over the past few years, as social media has become the main way many of us access information and share our views, there have been numerous examples of huge public outcry as a result of someone making a polarizing comment. Generally, these individuals were not deliberately aiming to be discriminatory. Mostly, they have used an unfortunate turn of phrase, they have inaccurately or poorly addressed someone, or they have been misinterpreted. However, the implications of 'cancel culture' are both toxic and unhealthy, not just in terms of the punishment and ostracizing of a person for one error in language, but for the fear it generates in broader society. Leaders in organizations see once popular figures in the media suddenly completely broken, and it immediately diminishes any courage they may have had to navigate the complexity of inclusion, for fear of the repercussions.

When I spoke on my podcast with Dr Pippa Grange, author of *Fear Less*, she highlighted another aspect of inclusive leadership that provokes this fear of complexity:

> The cultural way we've learned to perform at work doesn't give us much room to be flawed. It doesn't give us a lot of permission to not know; everything is reduced down to a deliverable or a key performance indicator. And this work just cannot

be that; it's not performance-based work. It's hard work; it's psychological work. And people are very anxious about being so exposed in that.

This is a really powerful statement on two levels. Firstly, Pippa helps identify an important issue about the way most performance systems are designed, which is that they are all about hitting targets and achieving the next big project. From the day we are born, we are constantly rewarded for doing things, whether it's taking our first step, getting to the top of a climbing frame or attaining excellent grades in school exams. We are assessed on the basis of what we do, and this is at the very core of how organizations utilize their people and make money. However, to Pippa's second point, inclusive leadership is about being, not doing. Leaders have to be willing to look at who they are, their views of the world, why they have those views and how they influence their interactions. But no one ever asks them to do this. Not only is it something they have never practised, but for the majority of leaders this psychological work is a fairly alien concept. When they do try to do this work, the complexity of the ideas they encounter can be overwhelming, to a point where they simply become frozen in discomfort and navigate their way back to what they know best.

 ## Creating safety for experimentation

It's important to acknowledge where you are on your journey to navigating the complexity of DEI, but equally where your colleagues are too. This means getting to know your fellow leaders and building strong relationships that are based on trust, psychological safety to share concerns or questions and willingness to approach each other when you get stuck.

As a DEI practitioner, I often find myself having to consciously hold back from offering answers, particularly when leaders are demonstrating Disconcerted, Proof-Seeking or Cheerleading behaviours. However, it isn't anybody's role to teach DEI to others. As a leader, your primary role is that of a guide. If you are always offering your views and your reality, it puts colleagues in a passive role as a receiver of information and promotes the binary bias that your reality is the truth.

Consider yourself to be a coach. Listen, observe, ask open questions and meet your colleagues where their need is. As is human nature, once we feel seen and heard, we feel safe to trust and experiment.

Expanding this Way of Being

When I reflect on my life so far, I notice a familiar pattern of setting ambitious goals and stopping at nothing to achieve them. As mentioned earlier, education was given high importance in my family, and so I studied and worked hard to gain a place at an all-girls grammar school, where I was a solid all-rounder. I achieved strong academic results, represented my school on various sporting teams and was head girl in sixth form. Everything in my environment was primed to reward my performance achievements – I learned that this is what success looked and felt like. All was set for me to study psychology at the University of Oxford, but my world came crashing down on results day when I realized my grades had slipped. Oxford wouldn't take me and, in a state of shock and disappointment, I went through an emotionally draining process of calling other universities to see if they had a space. I had other options of course: I could have resat my exams, found a job or gone off travelling with a friend. But, to me, all of these felt like failure. Why? Probably because I equated success with continuous onward progression. I had never learnt how to process the agonizing emotion of shame – I had never needed to. My self-confidence and self-worth took a painful blow and I just hadn't practised how to navigate this.

If, through reading this chapter, elements of a Cheerleading Way of Being have resonated with you, it's important to pause and reflect on what emotions are now present. How does the sudden awareness that you might not necessarily be as inclusive as you thought sit with you? Maybe it feels a bit like slipping grades? Does it make you question your leadership in the teams you have previously worked with, or wonder if team members felt like they didn't belong but you just didn't realize? In these moments, there can be an intense discomfort which bubbles away, attacking your self-worth as a leader and everything you thought you stood for. It is worth emphasizing at this point that my intention in this chapter is not to question your intentions for inclusion. Rather, I am offering an approach for achieving it.

So, what do you do with this discomfort and the guilt of shame that might be attacking your self-worth? Here, I guide you towards two people whose work has been so helpful to me in this area: Angela Lee Duckworth and Professor Carol Dweck.

In her famous TED Talk, Grit, psychologist and author Angela Lee Duckworth explains the importance of motivation in learning.[8] She studied children and adults in lots of challenging settings to understand the factors that influence success. For example, she researched students in a military academy, participants at the national Spelling Bee, less experienced teachers in rough neighbourhoods and salespeople in tough sales environments. She offers:

> In all those very different contexts, one characteristic emerged as a significant predictor of success. And it wasn't social intelligence, it wasn't good looks, physical health, and it wasn't IQ — it was grit. Grit is passion and perseverance for very long-term goals. Grit is having stamina. Grit is sticking with your future… for years. And working really hard to make that future a reality. Grit is living life as if it's a marathon, not a sprint.

This makes sense to me as an entrepreneur. I set up Avenir with the sole aim of making the world a more inclusive place. This purpose is ingrained in everything I do – in how I work with clients, in the products we develop, in what I post on social channels, in what I talk about in my keynotes and on my podcast show and in the painstaking process of writing the book you are currently reading. I believe with absolute conviction that the work I am doing contributes to my ultimate vision, and I recognize that the rewards aren't immediate. It's what keeps me going at the end of a particularly challenging workshop or when the world changes and I need to pivot to remain current and relevant.

Leaders who have a Cheerleading Way of Being need to find this grit within themselves. They have a solid foundation due to their existing motivation to enhance DEI, but they also need to accept when their current paths aren't serving their goals. Being able to let go of a deeply held belief system and start the marathon again, this time following a different course, is where this grit will really show through.

One way to obtain grit, as highlighted by Duckworth, is through a 'growth mindset'. Ever since my undergraduate degree, I have been fascinated by this concept and the work of Carol Dweck, Professor at Stanford University. In her TED Talk, she explains the power of shifting language and mindset from 'I've failed' to 'I can't do this yet': 'If you get a failing grade, you think "I'm nothing, I'm nowhere". But if you get the grade "not yet", you understand that you're on a learning curve. It gives you a path into the future.'[9] In her extensive research, Dweck found that a growth mindset was a distinguishing feature of those who could overcome challenge and difficulties, whereas those with a fixed mindset tended to give up.

There is no rule book for being an inclusive leader, no quick wins and no end point. In our 2023 research, *Unlocking Inclusive Leadership*, participants at the beginning of their learning journey expressed their struggle when trying to translate their positive attitudes around DEI into effective action:

I would like to improve my ability to have constructive conversations... calling out something I don't agree with or challenging someone's point of view... so that I'm doing it constructively, so it doesn't feel like I am on at them... and they don't get really defensive... it's a really difficult one to nail.[10]

You can hear the discomfort in this person's words, brought on by the risk of venturing onto an unknown path. Through the programme, we helped participants develop growth mindsets, creating a safe space where they could share, show their vulnerability and learn from each other. One participant shared their acceptance of the iterative learning process:

I don't think it [discomfort] ever goes away... someone said 'I have really sweaty palms', and I thought 'Snap!' You're definitely on high alert... but you just have to ride it and be like 'well, I'm uncomfortable for a reason and inherently that's a good reason'.

Those with a Cheerleading Way of Being have spent their lives and careers leading in ways that they felt were inclusive. If you recognize features of Cheerleading in yourself, reading the examples of invisible inequities either being missed or deliberately overlooked due to the belief it's best to see everyone the same would likely have been uncomfortable for you, to say the least. Just in case you fall into a binary bias here, I am not saying that you are a bad leader because you have this Way of Being. However, you might consider pressing the reset button on some of your existing beliefs about inclusion. In doing so, you will need both grit and a growth mindset. Notice the discomfort as you challenge yourself to see people's differences. What do you uncover by allowing yourself these observations? How does it change your actions and behaviour?

 Creating the right conditions

My experience of working with leaders is that they feel alone and unsupported in living up to everything that being an inclusive leader encompasses. One-off unconscious bias workshops tend to have little effect if there isn't a clear, practical application to the leaders' day jobs, and they can also lack impact when there isn't enough time for the leaders to create a sense of camaraderie or strength in numbers.

If your organization can spare the resources, offering a longer, more in-depth programme has numerous benefits. This can:

o   enable iterative learning and experimentation, trying a new Way of Being where there is opportunity and feedback;

o include role modelling for how to create a psychologically safe space where people are able to show their vulnerability and share personal stories, and feel truly seen and listened to – here, leaders receive first-hand experience of what this feels like so that they can replicate that feeling within their own teams;

o provide opportunity to create a shared understanding of what inclusive leadership is about and discover techniques that leaders have used to support each other's practice and development;

o instil a collective growth mindset, allowing participants to feel they are on a learning journey together and can call upon each other for support should they get stuck.

Chapter summary

In this chapter, I drew attention to the ultimate paradox presented by DEI – that in order for people to feel like they belong, you need to see their differences. Those with a Cheerleading Way of Being enjoy comfort by not seeing colour, gender or any other diversity characteristic. However, minimizing people's differences in this way serves not only to diminish the significance of their daily lived experiences of inequity, but also to avoid acknowledgement of leaders' own accountability in fuelling systems of injustice.

The challenge, of course, is that inequity is often invisible. I shed light on some of the many inequities, like skin tone and colour, social class, neurodiversity, accent and language, and fathering. All of these examples share a theme – we all have deeply embedded expectations of what is 'normal', and anyone who steps outside of these needs to quickly adapt to fit (which is not always possible) or they will pay the price. Those who are Cheerleading fear the complexity of treating people differently, because it is so intangible and because it goes against their current way of observing the world. How can we ever know if our leadership is fair? I ended the chapter by leaning on the work of Angela Lee Duckworth and Professor Carol Dweck, to encourage leaders to work through their discomfort through grit and a growth mindset.

Questions of discomfort

If, whilst reading this chapter, some of the Cheerleading perspectives resonated with you, you may find it helpful to use the questions below to further facilitate your thinking. Remember, you can download the free worksheet on the Beyond Discomfort website (www.beyond-discomfort.com).

o   How does it make you feel to consider that you are less inclusive than you thought you were? Where does this feeling stem from?

o   Think about a time when you felt you were treated unfairly because of certain rules or behaviours that favoured some people over others. What would a potential solution have been, to create equity?

o   How might you have benefited from inequities in society and organizational life?

o   If you were to focus on creating equity rather than equality, how would this change your past decisions?

o   Reflect on the diversity within your current (or past) team. How might the culture, norms and way things are generally done affect people in different ways? If you don't know, how could you find out?

o   If you were to accept the complexity of inclusive leadership and try anyway, what might this look like?

o   Reflect back on your life and pick out key moments when you have demonstrated grit – a passion and long-term perseverance for something. How might you apply this to your endeavour to be an inclusive leader?

o   On a scale of 1 to 10, where 1 is a fixed mindset and 10 is a growth mindset around being an inclusive leader, where would you place yourself, and why? What would need to be in place to support you in moving one or two notches up the scale?

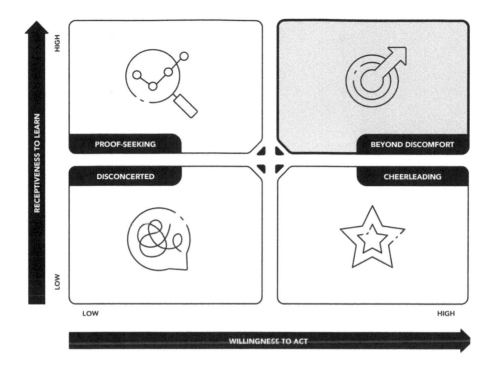

5 Beyond Discomfort

The only choice we have is to step up and show up, however imperfectly — to get comfortable with being uncomfortable. If you aren't pushing yourself to do more and pushing others around you to improve too, chances are, you aren't really leading.
                    —Jennifer Brown, author and inclusive leadership expert[1]

What makes leaders who have a Beyond Discomfort Way of Being unique is that they have broken free of society's traditional stereotypes of what a good leader should be. Their high Receptiveness to Learn about themselves, their privilege and their beliefs and biases means they understand the lens through which they see the world is different to everyone else's. They are prepared to tune in to their inner voice and challenge any unfair judgements and assumptions they are making about other people. They are open to having new conversations and, even though they might not fully understand every aspect of what they are told, their high Willingness to Act equitably and inclusively means they are prepared to be guided by what others tell them. They recognize the personal risks that showing this vulnerability carries and the often intense discomfort that this path takes, and they take it anyway.

It's worth noting that this doesn't mean that leaders with a Beyond Discomfort Way of Being won't at times be exclusionary. There will always be gaps in knowledge, understanding and analysis of actions. The difference, though, is that they are more likely to spot gaps, more practised at navigating the discomfort this presents and more adept at accepting the change they need to make in themselves and in their leadership.

In this chapter, I explain the courage and skill required to challenge systems of inequity effectively. I also discuss the courage needed to look inward and the psychological work required for continuous self-evaluation, showing vulnerability and being open to learning. I go on to explore what active allyship looks like and offer some tools to support a Beyond Discomfort Way of Being.

It takes courage

When my eldest daughter was six years old, I collected her from a playdate at a friend's house. On the way home, she started telling me about a game called 'Black Man', which her friend had taught her. The basic premise is that the children had to pretend there was a Black man hidden in some trees – or whatever suitable place was nearby – and as they walked towards the trees, someone would call out 'Black man' and they had to run away as fast as they could. I had to fight all my instincts in order to remain calm and curious. I enquired why they would run away. She responded: 'Because the Black Man is a villain, and he was trying to get us.' Tough parenting moment. We had a conversation about why associating the colour black with being bad, even as a game, might make some people with that skin colour feel upset and hurt. She listened and seemed to process this, and I silently congratulated myself for a conversation well handled. But then, after she shared this with a friend, came a question from the parent: 'Does the conversation need to extend beyond your daughter? Will there be more playdates?' I knew what they were getting at – I needed to have a conversation with the White mother of the child she had been playing with. But it wasn't that simple. If you have a child of primary school age, you'll know the politics that play out amongst parents. It can get surprisingly nasty, with each parent creating a protective barrier around their child. I wondered if this parent would likely interpret my words as 'your child is racist', which would not to go down well and could negatively impact how our family integrated at this new school. It was risky... too risky. I didn't say anything. If I had the chance, I would coach my former self to find the courage to speak to the mother and call in the game her kids were playing.

Challenging the system, whether it's one person or an organization, is scary, and often there is a lot at stake. Imagine you're a senior leader attending an industry dinner event with important clients. Wine is on tap and the drunken behaviour includes inappropriate sexual comments about the waitresses. What do you do? The discomfort often plays out on two levels: firstly, trying to find the best form of words to address the behaviour; and, secondly, the internal struggle of potentially jeopardizing current and future business relationships. It takes courage to say something, which will likely mean you will stick out and be on the receiving end of aggrieved and possibly aggressive people who will simply push you out of 'the circle' – you no longer belong because your views are different and you can't take a joke. It is also a developed skill to be able to select the most effective method to challenge in a given scenario.

In 2022, American music artist Lizzo made headlines when she used the term 'spaz' in her single release 'Grrrls'. The disability community called her out on this ableist term, which stems from 'spasticity', a medical condition where people lose control of their muscle movements. She responded immediately with an acknowledgement of her mistake and apology and she re-recorded the song with different lyrics. She explained: 'As a fat black woman in America, I've had many hurtful words used against me so I understand the power words can have.'[2] Her PR and media team were no doubt in a frenzy as a result of this call out, for fear that it would be the end of her career. However, Lizzo's courage in accepting her error coupled with her empathy of what it feels like to be abused and discriminated against made her more popular than ever.

Often, though, we don't have the luxury of having whole communities of people to back us up when we call out exclusionary behaviour. I recently facilitated a session for a group of 70 predominantly White, male senior leaders, some of whom knew each other very well and so there was a reasonable amount of comfort and lightness in the room. During a whole-group debrief, one male leader directed a heightist joke towards a fellow male colleague who was reasonably short in stature.

They both laughed, but I felt instant discomfort. As the facilitator, there was pressure to role model calling out exclusionary behaviour, but doing so in an environment with 69 of his peers might not go down so well. Admittedly, it was also a personal trigger for me, as being 5 foot 1 inch tall has made me the target of many height-related jokes in the past. So I had empathy. The conversation continued along the following lines.

'How might Paul [I checked his name tag] feel about your comment about his height?' I asked.

'Oh, Paul and I have worked with each other for 15 years; we know each other well. It's how we are with each other. He makes fun of me being so tall', he explained.

'How do you know that he doesn't feel hurt? It could be something he has constantly faced in his life and has learnt to brush off. But should he have to?' I challenged.

I looked at Paul, who was still smiling but in an awkward sort of way. He didn't step in to offer a contrary perspective, which I took as his way of confirming, at least in part, what I had said.

'He knows I don't mean anything by it. We are always making jokes at each other's expense.'

'And that might be OK if it's just the two of you. But what is the impact of doing it in front of all your peers?' I enquired.

He paused for a moment and said: 'Everyone here knows us well. They know what we're like.'

At that point, a female colleague challenged: 'Yes but what about all the other people who are short in this room. You don't know what people are carrying with them. Even though your comment was directed at Paul, it may have hurt others without you knowing.'

Boom. The penny dropped. I could see the intense discomfort in his face. He suddenly recognized the indirect consequences of his words and probably wanted the ground to swallow him. I noticed my own discomfort had presented in a rise in body temperature, beating heart and slightly shaking hands. That was tough. It had been risky. I was so grateful to the woman who had found the courage to be an upstander (as opposed to a bystander, only observing) and share her own views in validation of mine.

Whilst I don't profess to get this right all the time, it would be worth unpacking what I did on this occasion and why I chose the method I did. Let's first understand my options. We can think of addressing exclusionary behaviour on a continuum which spans from subtle to very direct. Very direct would be calling out what someone has said or done in the moment in a way that explicitly says what they have done wrong. The people who called out Lizzo were very direct, as are many of the examples you can think of where high-profile people have made inappropriate comments. In a business context, however, this very direct approach may be politically unsavvy, especially if you are a junior colleague calling out a more senior one or if you want to maintain positive relations. I chose not to use this method, out of respect for the public forum we were in as well as the sensitive position I was in as an external facilitator.

I follow the work of Loretta J. Ross, Professor at Smith College, who has started a 'calling in' movement, which offers a much more subtle way of challenging in order to create a learning opportunity rather than ostracize.[3] Calling in is done in private and with curiosity and respect. It is more of a two-way conversation of inquiry to help facilitate people's thinking about why their act could have been perceived as exclusionary. For example, imagine you're in a meeting to decide who to put forward for a new project, and a colleague makes a comment suggesting a team member, Gieta, who recently returned from maternity leave wouldn't be interested because it required a lot of travel. Calling in would be asking your colleague for a private conversation afterwards and saying: '*I'm interested in that comment you made about Gieta not wanting to travel. What makes you believe this is the case?*' The open question is subtle and therefore more likely to provoke thought rather than create a defensive response. So this may reveal a valid reason, based on what Gieta has said to them, or it may highlight that the person has made an assumption.

With Paul's colleague, I decided this calling in approach would be a less valuable learning opportunity for the whole group, as it would mean they wouldn't get to see how exclusionary behaviour could be addressed in a constructive way. Plus, I wasn't sure if I'd get an opportunity to speak to him in private afterwards. The approach I took was somewhere between subtle and very direct. I chose to role model inclusive leadership in the moment, in front of his peers, but did so with curiosity through my open questions, respectfully inviting him to reflect on his comment.

Regardless of the place on the continuum you decide to act from, it always involves discomfort and therefore always requires courage. A quote by Brené Brown, Professor at the University of Houston and author, says it all:

> *The greatest barrier to courageous leadership is not fear — it's how we respond to our fear. Our armor — the thoughts, emotions, and behaviors that we use to protect ourselves when we aren't willing and able to rumble with vulnerability — move us*

out of alignment with our values, corrode trust with our colleagues and teams, and prevent us from being our most courageous selves.[4]

It is psychological work

In the context of inclusive leadership, showing courage isn't just about calling in or calling out other people. It's about having the courage to look inwards with a deep curiosity to understand yourself. I'm not just talking about your personality type, food preferences or where you like to hang out on the weekend. This is about really seeing yourself – your values, your beliefs, the things that tend to annoy you and the things you admire or respect in others – recognizing your emotional triggers and asking yourself why you feel that way.

There's an activity we use in one of our workshops to help leaders with this process. We ask people to spend a few minutes thinking about the things they see in other people that really frustrate them, to a point where it becomes a distraction from what the person is saying or offering. Through the years, I have heard quite an eclectic list, from people not paying attention to grammar and punctuation before they send through their work to people who give a loose handshake, people who show up late for meetings, people with a visible tattoo and job candidates who walk into an interview with brown shoes! Whilst many of these are common 'niggles' for people, I had not been aware of any issue with brown shoes so I proceeded to find out more through three simple questions:

I started by saying to the participant: 'That's interesting. Where does that belief come from?'

'When I first started in the company, it just seemed to be a commonly held view. If a candidate had worn brown shoes to their interview, it was viewed as poor judgement and they wouldn't be taken seriously with brown shoes. And I noticed that all the sales consultants wore black shoes, so I guess I just adopted that perspective.'

My second question was: 'Is it possible that this belief doesn't apply all the time, every time?'

'Yes, I am sure there are very talented sales people out there who wear brown shoes and are great at their job.'

The third question I asked was: 'What might you be missing as a result of this belief?'

'I have probably missed out on some good people for my team.'

These three questions are powerful because they invite the person to pause and consider the roots of their beliefs. Often people respond by saying that it was something a parent or role model instilled in them as a child (for example, a work ethic or what it means to be professional) or it was drilled in at school. If you traced back the company view about brown shoes, it may have started with one senior leader having a bad experience with a new recruit who happened to wear this item of clothing – who knows? The point, though, is that it encourages the leader to question the validity of their beliefs, which turn out to be less grounded in fact than they might have previously thought.

By the end of the third question, if the person is open to self-evaluation, there is inevitably a level of discomfort through the self-acknowledgement that they haven't acted in a fair way and this has impacted someone else. That doesn't sit well with most of us. However, when I see a high Receptiveness to Learn in leaders, self-evaluation becomes part of their daily lives, in all their interactions and with a degree of scrutiny that doesn't paralyse them but offers continual insight into who they are. Leaders with a Beyond Discomfort Way of Being know that this process of digging deeper can uncover some aspects of who they are that don't necessarily align with their perceptions of self. They manage their fear of not being good enough, push away their 'armour' of self-protection and boldly self-reflect anyway.

Devi Virdi, Group Head of Diversity and Inclusion at Centrica, explained in our podcast discussion:

> Look, inclusion is actually tough, and it is a complex journey of truths. Because the reality is we still don't face those truths. And let's be honest, we are really uncomfortable with the truth and we are really uncomfortable with difference. This is important because in society, and in business, the reality is we need to own that truth as part of being human, as who we are, because if we don't own it, frankly, we're not going to get over it.

Let's think about some of these complex truths that Devi is talking about here:

o the truth that I hold biases and I regularly act on them without knowing;

o the truth that the beliefs I hold and the stories I hold run my life;

o the truth that I will tend to hold negative judgements about people who are different in some way;

o the truth that, every day, I contribute to the inequities in society and in my organization;

o   the truth that aspects of my background and who I am have influenced my successes and failures in life;

o   the truth that I am not always a good person.

It takes psychological work to process all these truths and what that then means. It can leave people in a place where they are questioning themselves as leaders and as people with integrity and morals. They may also be questioning whether their wins in life were really wins at all or simply the result of privilege playing out. Bear in mind that these questions don't invite 'once and done' answers. The more a leader enters this space of self-reflection and self-evaluation, the more discomfort they will feel as they realize how prevalent their bias and complicity in exclusion and discrimination is. Inclusive leaders need to sit with the constant discomfort that this awareness brings and resiliently continue down the never-ending path of deep inner work.

Marta Pajón Fustes, Head of Technical & Inclusion and Diversity at innocent drinks, summarized her experience of this on the *Why Care?* podcast:

> *The moment you start thinking about biases, you start triple thinking and, especially for people like me who tend to overthink, that is a challenge. Am I being fair here? Or is this my bias? You start questioning yourself more and more, and you have to be ready for that.*

 ### Overcoming resistance at the top

I have had many conversations with DEI leads or HR professionals who have been tasked with finding an appropriate supplier to run some unconscious bias or inclusive teams sessions across the business. My question is always: 'And how are the senior leaders engaging in this work?' Taking a 'sheep dip' approach to DEI training has never been and never will be the path to transformation. In my view, it is money down the drain.

If organizations are going to reap the business benefits of inclusion, you and fellow leaders must be willing to engage in the deep psychological work discussed in this chapter. This is challenging as it's unlikely that all the senior leaders will have a Beyond Discomfort Way of Being. More likely there will be a mix of Proof-Seeking, Disconcerted and Cheerleading Ways of Being, with all these types resisting fully engaging in the work.

It's important to recognize people's fear of facing into all their truths, which many others will see as a flaw in leadership. The key is to take small steps in the psychological work. Start with a discussion on your values and gain alignment across the executive team. Encourage everyone to connect your shared values with the DEI endeavour. Often the resistance comes from the discomfort of not knowing what you are doing. Organize educational, content-driven, bite-size learning sessions so you all feel more equipped to move forwards through better understanding. Look out for external events or bring in speakers so you can feel inspired by leaders who are already engaging Beyond Discomfort.

Leader as learner

What sets a Beyond Discomfort leader apart from others is that they have a willingness to share their discoveries – both about themselves and what they notice in the world – as they live them, with openness, honesty and raw vulnerability. They allow people to witness their struggles or lack of understanding first-hand, thereby creating permission for others to do the same. In January 2023, Jacinda Ardern, New Zealand's Prime Minister through the global pandemic, resigned. Her speech beautifully illustrates her value for sharing with honesty:

> I'm leaving, because with such a privileged role comes responsibility – the responsibility to know when you are the right person to lead and also when you are not. I know what this job takes. And I know that I no longer have enough in the tank to do it justice. It's that simple.[5]

I wonder how many other leaders have been in the same position as Jacinda and either battled on through, believing that showed strength and resilience, or resigned in silence? Unlike leaders with a Proof-Seeking Way of Being, who analyse the world based on their existing premises and beliefs, Beyond Discomfort leaders take a more experimental approach to leadership in the spirit of continuous learning and evolution. Disney's *Monsters, Inc.* offers a helpful analogy here. In the film, the monsters have a long-standing belief that getting children to scream is the only way to generate electrical power. But as Sulley and Mike (the two main characters) discover when they take care of a young girl, her laughter generates far more energy. In a similar way, despite the widely held view of what strong leadership means and many examples of archetypal leadership qualities bringing success, inclusive leaders are willing to try a different approach – one that is hugely stretching and uncomfortable but which can be much more powerful. The only way to find out is to take the risk that comes with authenticity and vulnerability.

In my interview in 2023 with Faran Johnson, Chief People Officer at Motor Insurers' Bureau, she explained what is distinct about a Beyond Discomfort leader: 'They're open enough to say: "*I'm not perfect. So, I might say things in the wrong way, I might use the wrong words, I might ask questions that will show me to be perceptually ignorant about something, but I'm doing it from a place of wanting to learn.*"' It's worth noting that if leaders are operating in an environment where there is fear of being 'cancelled', the chances of seeing the behaviours Faran describes are minimal. Psychological safety is key to leading Beyond Discomfort, which requires the most senior leaders to role model behaviour so as to 'give permission' to others to do the same (more on this in Chapter 6).

A Beyond Discomfort leader has managed to unravel themselves from the boundaries of what a leader should be, which in turn means relinquishing the deep desire to feel competent and be right. Think of a time in a meeting when you were asked a question that you didn't know the answer to. There's a physiological response that usually comes with the pressure to respond – you might start to feel a bit warm and sweaty, your heart might beat faster, your breathing might quicken and you might feel the rush of blood to your face. Now imagine being free of the expectation to have the answer. This isn't easy, because everything we have read, seen and practised about being a good leader suggests that we should feel bad about ourselves for not knowing. Of course, there are times when you are the technical expert in the room and so having an answer is part of your job. This isn't the sort of situation I'm talking about. I'm referring to opportunities you may have to sponsor an employee network or resource group you don't personally identify with, or join a panel discussion on a DEI topic that is unfamiliar to you. It's natural to find this sort of situation deeply uncomfortable, yet it's important to overcome any visceral response with a learner mindset.

With a high Receptiveness to Learn, inclusive leaders are able to sit with the discomfort of asking questions about someone else's lived experience as well as the inner tension of hearing and processing a perspective that is hugely at odds with their own. As learners, they are forgiving and compassionate towards themselves for not realizing that alternative realities and different truths exist. With time and practice, the 'leader as learner' mindset is incredibly rich and fulfilling, as well as challenging and uncomfortable, as they expand their viewpoint and see all the nuances of each decision and each word they speak.

On my podcast, Charlotte Cox, President EMEA for Pentland Brands, shared what she has learned over her career as a leader with regards to the value that diversity brings:

> As leaders, we know we often don't have all the right answers, and we just need to be honest about that and really own it and accept that we need different perspectives to provide a solution that's far better than we could have probably come up with ourselves… Leaders have to step into it because it requires effort… and it requires thoughtfulness to set that up.

 ### Assessing organizational maturity

There is a wealth of initiatives you could delve into that will support education and learning on DEI. For example, hosting webinars or 'lunch and learns' around some of the annual events and national days/months celebrating minority groups is a powerful way of sharing statistics and stories to put a spotlight on inequities. You could also set up employee resource groups or staff networks, where people can talk about issues and experiences faced by a particular identity.

Before doing so, however, it's important to assess what your organization is ready for. Here are some helpful questions for you to reflect on:

o Where do you feel you and your leadership colleagues lie in the Beyond Discomfort® model? How ready is everyone for uncomfortable conversations? How able are you all to share your own stories and receive others?

o   How trusting are staff in the integrity of the organization and its DEI endeavour? Do you hear undercurrents of cynicism – for example, the notion that this is just a tick-box exercise?

o   How safe do staff feel to share their lived experiences and different perspectives in an open forum without fear of negative repercussions?

Remember that safety and trust are integral to DEI maturity. If your organization isn't quite there yet, then you need to be mindful to create a strong foundation for DEI rather than jumping ahead too quickly. For example, if you are setting up a race and cultural heritage network, it may be best, initially, if it were only open to people who identify as being in a racial minority. Once the group is well established and there is more trust in the organization's DEI goals and in the leaders, you can then encourage expansion of the network to allies – that is, people who are in the racial majority but want to learn and support the pursuit of racial equity. After that, even greater maturity would be blending the networks to achieve an intersectional lens and develop even more meaningful conversations.

Leading the action

When I meet a leader with a Beyond Discomfort Way of Being, there is something both inspiring and compelling about them which is a result of them leading from the heart and with clarity of purpose. They have connected with the reason why DEI is important to them personally, and to the world, and this propels them forward with a high Willingness to Act.

A high-profile example of this is tennis icon Andy Murray, who has an extensive list of moments when he has publicly displayed his outrage on gender inequality and his active support of sportswomen. In 2016, he was congratulated for being the first person to win two Olympic tennis gold medals, to which he promptly responded: 'I think Venus and Serena [Williams] have won about four each.'[6] He has challenged the scheduling of matches where lower-seeded men's matches were played on more prestigious courts than higher-seeded women's matches. Notably, he is one of the few top sportsmen to hire a female coach, calling out the harsher treatment she received when he lost a match compared to her male predecessor. It's clear that his allyship to women and drive to create equality has personal meaning for him. He often speaks about his mother and grandmothers as powerful influencers in his life.

Let's explore what I mean by allyship here, as there are, broadly speaking, two forms – performative and active. Performative allyship is where people attend events, like or share other people's posts or wear something as a symbol of their support, but they aren't actually changing anything about how they lead and aren't encouraging change in their organization either. This is easy and comfortable. Performative allyship differs vastly from active allyship as demonstrated by the actions of Andy Murray, who is speaking up, writing posts on social channels and using his influencer status to make change happen and support a community.

There is, of course, an important distinction between active allyship and saviourism. An active ally does not believe they know better than the community they are supporting and does not speak on behalf of them. A saviour, despite their positive intent, is acting in the comfort of their power, falling into a familiar relational dynamic where they limit the agency of those they are trying to help. Marc McKenna-Coles, currently Head of Inclusion & Diversity at easyJet, describes how he walks the line of active allyship:

> I talk about being a trans ally. And I think, as a gay man, I feel that I should be. I have a lot of friends who are part of the trans community, but I also think that I've wanted to learn. I had some insecurities around gender identity in the past – I didn't understand why someone identified in a particular way. I now understand a huge amount more. I don't think I understand it all, because I'm not a trans person myself, I'm a cisgender male, but I don't ever speak on behalf of the trans community. What I will do is speak alongside the trans community.

There is also a more subtle, but by no means less vital, aspect to leading the action which relates to how the leader creates psychologically safe spaces for people to share. The term 'psychological safety' was brought to mainstream attention by Amy Edmundson, author of The Fearless Organization and Novartis Professor of Leadership and Management at Harvard Business School. In the book, she says: 'Psychological safety exists when people feel their workplace is an environment where they can speak up, offer ideas, and ask questions without fear of being punished or embarrassed.'[7] This feeling of safety is crucial to inclusion. People need to feel like their voice will be heard if they choose to offer an alternative perspective, and that there won't be negative repercussions in doing so. But it does not happen by chance.

What sets leaders with a Beyond Discomfort Way of Being apart from all other leaders is being connected to their humanity. They share what deeply moves or touches them, they reach out with empathy when someone is in pain, and they acknowledge mistakes. They recognize that people need to see this authenticity in order to feel safe to share in return.

Many leaders, like Eric Pliner, Chief Executive of YSC Consulting (now part of Accenture), partially lost sight of this humanity at the start of the Covid-19 pandemic when there was significant pressure and focus on business survival. In one of the most widely listened to *Why Care?* episodes, he talked about recognizing what he had lost in his leadership and how he regained his connection with staff during lockdown:

> We had no sense of each other beyond the small snippet of backdrop that we could see on our screens. And so really listening to what everybody's day-to-day lives were like and sharing a bit about my own... talking openly about what my challenges and my energizers were, and getting the same from the people around me as a part of my regular day-to-day work was the way that I began to re-engage legitimately with our teams.

As Eric shared his story with me, I noticed something more powerful than simply the words he was saying. There was emotion there and I could feel it. Inclusion is a core part of who a leader is, not just what the leader does. It becomes less of an active choice and more of a compelling drive to do whatever it takes for equity, fairness and justice. Having said that, we can't all be active allies on the same scale and impact as Andy Murray, and that certainly isn't the measure of a Beyond Discomfort leader. There are times where a small action can make a huge difference in how valued, seen and included someone feels.

A note to DEI practitioners

Most DEI practitioners would openly acknowledge that they didn't fully appreciate how tough the role is when they entered the arena. Firstly, we carry our own biases, which we have to constantly practise awareness and management of, and even though we know there is no way to be right all the time, we still give ourselves a hard time when we don't know the answer. Secondly, where people's response to what you are teaching or offering is partly based on your identity, there's a constant need to navigate a path through facilitation and coaching.

In our discussion on the *Why Care?* podcast, Errol Amerasekera, a man from a minority ethnic background, explained:

> For obvious reasons, I find working with race challenging. Because as soon as a topic of racism comes up, I feel like I'm in a low power spot. The challenge is how do I acknowledge that and then simultaneously access my power as a facilitator and my awareness as a coach and leader, and have both of those simultaneously?

And of course, the same challenge would play out for facilitators who don't identify with a particular marginalized group but are facilitating discussions with people who have experienced oppression.

As a facilitator, I have felt the tension when creating a safe space for participants to be open about their perspectives yet feeling personally triggered by what they have to say. I have completed workshops feeling emotionally exhausted. In the same podcast episode, Dr Pippa Grange reflected on the complexity of this work: 'It's slow and intense. It's not going to be fixed tomorrow. It's dynamic in its orientation rather than something we're going to finish. And we have to do it kindred – together, in friendship and community.' For me, this is the foundation of an outstanding DEI practitioner. I am thankful each day for my network of fellow practitioners, who offer me strength, support and sanity in the messiness of DEI that I navigate in work and life.

Supporting this Way of Being

Consistently having a Beyond Discomfort Way of Being is tough. Think about everything that's discussed in this chapter – this is someone who has the courage to call in or call out exclusionary behaviour, who can look deeply at the world around us and see the grim reality that it holds and also manage the inner tension of their contribution to this and be able to show their vulnerability in service of learning. They must be able to critically evaluate their pre-existing beliefs and values continuously and with an open mind that allows them to reassess their truths. Simultaneously, they need to reconcile their discoveries with their sense of self, noticing how this is evolving through acknowledging both the good and not so good aspects of who they once were, and still might be.

This was beautifully illustrated by Claire Brody, Director, DEI, EMEA at Warner Bros. Discovery:

> I'm a White, LGBT woman. I grew up in a small town in East Texas where White was not the majority in school. My parents raised me, but I was also raised by

a Black mother. And I think growing up and having such an appreciation for Black culture, I always thought, 'Oh, I'm one of the good ones.' But just because I have had the opportunity of being exposed to, and developed an appreciation for, Black culture from a young age, it doesn't absolve me of my White identity or privilege... That's been an incredibly uncomfortable journey, to say, actually, I'm not 'one of the good ones'; that's not something that exists. Every single day, it's really a journey for me to deconstruct and unlearn the things that I believe to be true, understand the systems that I operate within and benefit from, and really think about what that journey of self-awareness and allyship is.

A daily practice. Like waking up in the morning and brushing your teeth. Except you're never really sure when the practice will be needed. It could be when you feel alert as a Black man walks behind you in the street on your commute to work, or when you note you are deliberately avoiding a work colleague who has multiple sclerosis, or when you realize your direct report has been struggling with the spreadsheets you have been sending them due to their dyscalculia. The list is endless because we are endlessly making assumptions, judgements and decisions each and every day. This is why living Beyond Discomfort needs continuous support and reinforcement.

Over the past decade, we have seen an increase in the number of people talking about mental health, self-care and living a wholesome life, whether it is related to mindfulness practice, eating well or general daily exercise (I am a huge fan of Fern Cotton and Dr Rangan Chatterjee for their accessible approach on these topics[8]). Our watches now buzz to tell us off for not moving enough each hour, and we have apps on our phones to remind us to take five minutes to switch off from the intensity of our work. There's a reason for this, which is related to a growing disconnect between mind and body. I see this in my coaching practice too – I ask coachees a question about how they feel, but they can only tell me their analysis of what they think is happening. For example, I might say, *'Tell me what it feels like to be ignored in that way'*, and my coachee will reply, *'Don't get me wrong, I don't think they are doing it on purpose.'* It's actually quite odd to ask a question and get a completely unrelated answer, but it happens regularly. Not only are leaders unaware of their emotions, but often they are well practised at pushing them into a tiny box and sealing them up with some heavy-duty tape.

As we know, leading Beyond Discomfort is the antonym of this – it is leading with an open heart. Even if this style of leadership comes naturally to you, in this fast-paced, always-on culture we are now living in it is so easy to solely focus on tasks and deadlines and forget to pause. This pause is crucial to supporting an inclusive leader – firstly, because only then can we truly listen to our inner voice and start challenging its assumptions and, secondly, because it offers us space to dissect the meaning behind what we have noticed in ourselves.

Jon Kabat-Zinn has supported the development of a mindfulness technique of 'centring and grounding', which I often use with my coachees to help direct their attention away from their heads to their emotions and bodies.[9] Through focusing solely on breathing, centring helps people notice the tensions they are holding and direct energy to the centre of the body to create clarity and calm. Grounding dials up people's sensory awareness, connecting them with their surroundings and bringing their attention to where they are in the present. Practising this for two minutes each morning whilst acknowledging your intention to lead Beyond Discomfort in the day ahead would make a significant difference.

But, I am a realist, and I know that these techniques aren't for everyone, whether you believe they work or not. Pause can come in many different forms, though, including from physical exercise, yoga, going for a walk and quiet reflection. Use the time to reflect on moments of discomfort when perhaps you're trying to avoid an inner struggle or uncertainty related to DEI. In cognitive behavioural therapy, there is a technique known as 'acceptance and commitment', developed by University of Nevada Professor Steven Hayes, which supports you to listen to your self-talk and accept the discomfort for what it is whilst you work through a way to navigate the issue.[10] What do you need to say to yourself that will help you accept the emotions you're experiencing about this particular DEI situation? For example, earlier on I described my inner turmoil about addressing the Black Man game. I might have said to myself: 'I'm *scared of rejection and the potential consequences of speaking up, and that's OK because it comes from wanting to belong.*' Being present in my feelings and acknowledging them without judgement is important. Through being centred and grounded, I can then distance myself from the emotions and focus on what is important to me (my values). I might then have said to myself: '*Your inclusive values mean that you won't be able to let this go until you have addressed it.*' This offers me a choice – to be guided by my emotion of fear or by my values – and, subsequently, a decision on what to do – say something or say nothing.

Alongside this independent support you can offer to yourself, you can also build collective resilience through finding a few people in your organization who are on the same leadership endeavour as you. In our *Unlocking Inclusive Leadership* research, we found that one of the powerful byproducts of our inclusive leadership programme is that leaders felt they were 'in it together'. By the end of the programme, participants are usually calling upon each other to help think through and navigate both work and personal DEI-related situations. For many, it comes as a welcome relief that they don't have to work through this complexity on their own.

Supporting psychological safety

As a leader, it isn't your sole responsibility to create a psychologically safe organization, but there are ways you can both encourage and support it:

o Organize facilitated sessions where you and other leaders can reflect on teams you have worked in where you felt safe and those where you didn't. Pull out themes from your examples to help make psychological safety more tangible for everyone.

o At the beginning and end of workshops, you and your colleagues can rate how comfortable you feel sharing your views in the group, on a scale of 0 to 10. Then debrief on why your scores changed (or didn't) over the course of the workshop – reflect and share what experiences led to your scoring the way you did.

o Participate in panel events where you and other leaders openly share your stories, say why DEI is important to you and describe when you have and haven't got it right. This vulnerability and openness will support others to feel they can do the same.

o Run a series of 'lunch and learn' sessions, where people either discuss a pre-set DEI-related article or bring a current news piece to share and gather opinions on. This role models how people can come together, debate and offer different perspectives.

Chapter summary

In this chapter, I explored the deep inner work of inclusive leadership. As a leader, you will come across DEI-related situations in your daily life. Naturally, the more you read and develop your awareness of DEI, the more you will realize how intertwined your leadership challenges are with the concepts, and the more challenged you will feel. It takes courage to speak up, call in or call out exclusionary behaviour, especially when there is personal risk involved, perhaps related to how people perceive you or your job. The psychological work is about recognizing your own biases and assumptions, listening to your self-talk and continuously challenging yourself. You also need to navigate the emotions that inevitably arise when you process what these biases say about you as a leader.

Leading Beyond Discomfort means showing vulnerability about not having all the answers and inviting other people to guide you through sharing their truths, which you may have previously been unaware of. Being an ally means walking alongside people of a marginalized community and actively demonstrating support whilst knowing that it may leave you open to criticism from others who have different views. Finally, I shared mindfulness techniques of centring and grounding as a way of taking pause in your day and supporting a Beyond Discomfort Way of Being.

Exercises of discomfort

The reflective exercises below aim to support and develop a Beyond Discomfort Way of Being. There a number of free worksheets on the Beyond Discomfort website (www.beyond-discomfort.com) to guide you through each of these practices. You may find it valuable to share and learn together with your colleagues or team members.

o Reflect on a time when you have observed or heard exclusionary behaviour but didn't say or do anything. What were the factors that contributed to this decision? Write a list of external factors and those related to your beliefs and emotions.

o Now consider a time when you have demonstrated courage to call in or call out exclusionary behaviour or processes. What was different to the first situation (again, consider internal and external factors)?

o For just one day, be more alert to other people's truths. In conversation with colleagues, friends and family, notice the language people use and how it offers insights into their beliefs. Then do the same exercise on yourself.

o Reflect on ways you demonstrate allyship to a community, and notice where they sit on the scale of performative to active allyship. What actions feel less comfortable for you and why? What would need to happen for you to take a more vocal and active approach?

o Connect with and talk to a leader you admire for their inclusive approach. Find out more about their practice. For example, what do they struggle with and how do they manage this? What deeper psychological work have they had to do, and what have they learnt about themselves?

o   Actively place a five-minute pause in your day for the sole intention of centring and grounding. Select the approach that works for you and practise regularly. Use this practice to support you in slowing down your decision-making, with an active intention to be inclusive.

o   Find one or two peers in your organization who similarly want to develop their inclusive approach and who you feel safe sharing your experiences with. Lean on each other to share moments of difficulty, where the most inclusive solution is unclear or when you have learnt something about yourself which makes you feel uneasy or unsure.

6   Your organization Beyond Discomfort

Change is uncomfortable and as hard as hell. When leaders expect others to change without participating + holding themselves accountable – it's almost impossible. When leaders show up and model the vulnerability required for transformation change – it's often unstoppable.
         —Brené Brown, research professor, author and podcast host[1]

Imagine an organization where the chief executive and top team are all leading Beyond Discomfort. They offer safe spaces for people to share their perspectives, inquire with genuine curiosity to learn about employees different experiences, are open to dismantling processes and systems so they are more equitable, actively bring in diverse talent that reflects their market, are transparent about what they don't get quite right and hold managers accountable when they don't see the same. You can see how this would be an incredible organization to work for and also how it would stand out from its competitors. If you know an organization with a top team like this, please drop me a line – without doubt, they are few and far between.

Here is the more familiar story that I come across. The enhanced focus on DEI as a result of the global pandemic, the Black Lives Matter movement, the greater openness in certain societies around the LGBTQ+ community and greater awareness of mental health, disability and neurodiversity has been unsettling for senior leaders. They can feel tension in their organizations and the expectation that unspoken DEI issues will be identified and dealt with – but how? They find someone in the organization who has a passion for DEI (typically who identifies with a marginalized group) and will squeeze it into their day job, or they create a full- or part-time DEI position. Or they might hand it to the HR lead because DEI is about people. This individual then has responsibility to put in place unconscious bias training for staff (which the top team don't have time to attend) and has a remit to focus on increasing representation across the organization, even though everyone knows it isn't something one person alone can achieve. That this is just lip service to DEI is clear to all who work there, and it invokes an unhealthy cynicism. And because the focus is on awareness-raising rather than changing behaviours or mindsets, progress is minimal and any early momentum is lost.

It takes time and stamina to create an organization that operates Beyond Discomfort, has a deeply embedded Receptiveness to Learn and is open to taking itself apart and reassembling itself in a different way for the benefit of all. Its Willingness to Act isn't driven by a threat to the organization's reputation, but instead through a desire to push the boundaries of what inclusion looks like so that everyone can be at their best.

In this chapter, I explain the fundamentals of an organization Beyond Discomfort, which stems from a collective and genuine desire to achieve inclusion across all senior leaders together with a clear, data-led DEI strategy. I share examples of how organizations have put DEI at the heart of what they do, which is visible in their values and what they stand for. I also explore the additional complexities of DEI at a global scale and offer actions you can take to facilitate your organization's journey Beyond Discomfort.

Go deep, tackle culture

I was recently on a call with a potential client – a managing director of a global health services company which had seen rapid growth, within just a few years, from just a handful of people to over two hundred employees. The managing director explained that he wanted a quick intervention, as they were starting to get more issues related to racism, sexism and use of exclusionary language and were seeing more complaints taken to HR and higher staff turnover than before. He needed to gain buy-in from the other executive team members for the DEI work, and he thought it would be easier if this had a gender equality focus, as sexism was a widespread global issue for the organization. It was the 'lowest-hanging fruit' so to speak, and whilst by no means an easy option, it would be easier to sell and create a narrative around this. I have heard this logic on several occasions and, for me, it skirts around the discomfort of digging into the depths of an organization's culture to truly understand the root cause of its issues. The first step is almost inevitably engaging with the executive team and key stakeholders to gauge their appetite for the psychological inner work – at both individual and organizational levels. Focusing on gender as a starting point is a symptom-led approach. I explained to the managing director that although it would take a little longer, a data-led approach would mean we could learn about the current experiences and realities of people who worked in the organization, and this might guide us elsewhere. After all, you can't decide which direction to head towards if you don't know where you're starting from. Despite my prevailing logic, I never heard back, and I assume he found another consultancy firm that was willing to offer the solution he was seeking.

The other common 'go-to' starting point for organizational DEI work is to focus on de-biasing the recruitment process. This is often a reaction to either not getting enough diversity in the candidate pool or a having a limited number of new hires from underrepresented groups. I'm not denying that bias in recruitment is a problem and there is certainly work most organizations can do to prevent the mirrortocracy or affinity bias discussed in Chapter 2. What I am challenging is the premise that this should be where organizations start. Let's imagine that more diverse talent enters the organization, but without any preparatory work about how their colleagues and managers will receive them. They will very quickly feel segregated and will likely hide aspects of their differences through the desire to fit in. When no one seems to be meeting them halfway, they leave. Paulo Gaudiano offered a helpful analogy in our podcast discussion:

> Imagine that I was in the house and my wife came to me and said, 'Oh, honey, it's so cold – look, the thermometer only reads 11 degrees centigrade.' And I say, 'I'll fix that', and I light a match under the thermostat, and now look, the thermostat reads 25 degrees. Meanwhile the windows are open, the door is broken and the roof is leaking. When we try to stuff diverse employees, especially at the entry level, that's all you're doing – you're not fixing the problem, you're fixing the symptoms.

The benefit of focusing on achieving diversity as an *outcome* of inclusion, aside from retaining diverse talent, is that it can allay some of the concerns around unfairness. For example, if the organization leads with the narrative that they are trying to address the issue of having too few minority individuals, particularly at senior levels, it's understandable that those in the majority will feel like they aren't wanted any more. On the other hand, if the organization leads with sharing the real experiences of those in the minority, from the overt cases of discrimination to the subtle comments and acts of exclusion, most people will agree that action needs to be taken to address the culture. Setting representation targets and de-biasing the recruitment process can then be framed as methods the organization is adopting to achieve the bigger-picture end goal. In other words, people are more likely to buy into creating a positive culture where everyone can thrive, compared to action that looks like some people will lose out to benefit the greater good – this won't wash. It never will.

The journey towards an organization Beyond Discomfort must start with the top team, because they set the tone for the organization's culture. Not just one or two members, but all of them. They need to be collectively willing to peel back every layer of the organization to see what is below the surface, no matter how shocking the discoveries. They need to recognize how the current systems, processes and policies have historically served certain types of people (including themselves) more than others and seek to make the necessary changes. They need to all be aligned on the view that DEI is core to their business performance so that, even during times of crisis, it never falls off their board meeting agenda. They need to expend time and effort, both individually and collectively, to make their organizational DEI commitments reality and empower others to do the same. And all this work needs to be visible to the whole organization.

Alex Howard Group is an international group of therapeutic, health and nutrition organizations. Over a period of several months, I worked with their top 16 leaders, opening up new discussions on uncomfortable DEI topics and creating a safe space for them to consider how to apply inclusive leadership in their respective roles. One year later, I touched base with them and felt uplifted to observe an organization practising Beyond Discomfort. Their regular DEI Committee is attended by the CEO, and it discusses progress on their DEI strategy and new ways to embed DEI in the organization's processes, policies and decision-making. Notably, they had also acknowledged their accountability to increasing diversity in a mainly White, middle-class industry through establishing minority ethnic and social mobility scholarship programmes. Their course notes, materials and online content are continuously reviewed to ensure inclusive language and to create better representation of how health challenges are experienced. In essence, they are digging deeper into every aspect of their internal and external offering and are prepared to rebuild their foundations. When I interviewed Alex Howard, CEO and Founder, in 2023, he explained: 'There have been several uncomfortable moments of realization along the way of course. But we collectively decided to be part of the solution, not part of the problem, which means actively pursuing substantial change in our industry.'

Broadly speaking, industries that typically rank the highest for DEI tend to be those that historically have had the most homogeneous work environments, such as healthcare (for example, Sodexo, Johnson & Johnson, Invitae), technology (for example, Salesforce, Asana, Slack), professional services (for example, Accenture, McKinsey & Co) and finance (for example, Citigroup, Blackrock). However, there are other historically homogenous industries where progress in DEI has been painfully slow, such as law, construction, the armed forces and professional sport. I believe a key distinguishing factor between the companies at the top and those at the bottom of lists such as Glassdoor's Best Places to Work is senior leaders' collective and sustained focus and drive for change. Where the aspiration is clear and consistently role modelled by senior leaders, it inspires change throughout.

Creating a DEI committee and champions

You'll find that so many employees are passionate about DEI and want to get involved in the work. Not only is it important for the organization to recognize and utilize this untapped energy, but arguably cultural change can't happen without these individuals. Creating a DEI committee which is sponsored by an active senior leader is a great way to establish a call to action. It can be open to anyone in the organization and can have the dual purpose of creating space for people to share and discuss DEI topics whilst also delivering the organization's DEI strategy. Make sure there are clear delivery goals with a mechanism to report progress to senior leadership. This is key to sustaining engagement, as people will feel energized by the visibility of their work.

Several of my clients have also identified DEI champions or ambassadors. These are people on the ground, in each office location, who can observe, respond to DEI questions or requests for support, and collectively offer a sense of the wins to be celebrated and challenges to be worked on. For this to be successful, it is worth considering the following:

o   having a clear profile for this role with defined responsibilities;

o   having an executive sponsor who meets with the champions regularly and then discusses themes with the leadership team;

o   offering DEI training to build the knowledge and confidence of individuals in the role;

o   engaging with the champions' line managers so that the role forms part of their overall deliverables rather than being an add on;

o   finding a way to reward or compensate the champions for the additional duties. This doesn't have to be in monetary form; rather, this might involve giving them visibility with senior leaders, enabling them to attend high-profile DEI events and formalizing their role so they can add it to their LinkedIn page and CV.

Transparency and providing direction

So far we have seen that inclusion and belonging can't be achieved by solely focusing on diversity, but it is also true that change can't be achieved unless measured. To illustrate, in 2017, BBC TV presenter Ros Atkins started the 50:50 Project. The idea was sparked following a long car journey in which he suddenly became aware that he hadn't heard a single female voice on any radio show for a decent length of time. Ros set up the 50:50 Project as a way of actively monitoring how BBC coverage represented society. In our podcast discussion, Nina Goswami, who previously worked as the Creative Diversity Lead on the project, explained:

> We count the number of men and number of women on our programmes to see if we can reach 50% women over a month. So that allows for ebbs and flows in news cycles – you might be doing a story that is female heavy one day and male heavy another day. By understanding what the data says, we can better represent women on our programme, and we can provide better storytelling by enriching our content with different voices.

Interestingly, the BBC didn't make the 50:50 Project mandatory for all teams across the organization. Nina described it as a 'pincer movement' where non-participating producers and editors started to see changes in female representation in a few of the programmes that had signed up to the project, and decided to join in. By 2022, they had 750 teams all counting their numbers, sharing their figures and actively seeking out more female representation. 'For those who have been in the project for four years or more, 69% of teams reached 50% women, compared to 31% when they first joined', Nina shared.

The 50:50 Project is still going strong and has many external partners signed up globally. Several factors contribute to its success. Firstly, the process of measuring representation is very simple to encourage voluntary action, and if organizations struggle to collect the data, they can access support and advice. Secondly, seeing the representation figures acts as a driver and motivator for change. The transparency of data alerts people to how their actions are contributing to the lack of representation, and they are given a clear process for how to create change. Thirdly, they are rewarded through seeing a shift in consumer market data, demonstrating how their active work has a direct impact on increasing the diversity of their audience and enhancing programme quality. In summary, the process provides data-led reasoning for monitoring representation and offers evidence of a clear benefit to the business bottom line to help drive, sustain and grow the focus, attention and energy of the DEI work.

Creating an organization Beyond Discomfort, like any culture transformation programme, must have a vision of the future and a strategy to get there. I often find that leaders are overwhelmed by the volume of potential DEI work, confused about which of the multiple approaches to take and unclear how to prioritize their time and resources. This can either create a chaotic scattergun approach, trying to do too much and achieving very little, or stall decision-making so nothing happens at all. Clearly neither is favourable. There is only one place to start, and that's with a DEI strategy that is based on organizational data and has a robust narrative sitting behind it that everyone understands and supports.

In my experience of supporting our client organizations to develop their DEI strategy, the key to success has always started with the CEO delivering an open and transparent message to their staff about what the current data shows. This is powerful because it shows vulnerability in stating what the organization isn't good at, builds credibility through owning the data and creates a psychological contract with employees in terms of its commitment to learning more and doing something about it. Typically, we then invite all staff to a series of webinars, with the main intention of creating collective understanding of what DEI is, generating energy for the work and informing of them of their involvement in the next steps. It is important that everyone feels like they are part of the change.

A DEI strategy should be grounded in the specific needs of the organization. The only way to make this diagnosis is to analyse the organization's 'central nervous system' — that is, understand the experiences of everyone who works there. For example, you could run an inclusion survey to gain a 'line in the sand' and provide vital insights across socio-demographic groups, such as majority versus minority ethnic backgrounds, people with a disability compared to those without, and so on. Data often reveals uncomfortable truths, and I have seen a whole raft of responses by executive leaders to survey insights; these range from denial and defensiveness to inquisitiveness and embracingness. Arguably even more uncomfortable is owning the data and sharing it across the organization. But transparency is crucial for trust and belief, and the sustained action that follows is key to dispelling cynicism and engendering collective momentum to change.

Hearts and minds

There is an increasing number of influential DEI advertising campaigns sponsored by leading brands that evoke emotion and stimulate thought and dialogue. A few that spring to mind are: Always' #LikeAGirl, Dove's #ShowUs, Mercedes-Benz's Be One of Many and Starbucks' #ItStartsWithYourName. This type of storytelling campaign is marketers' way of influencing consumers to connect with a brand and feel a sense of shared values, in order to enhance brand reputation.

In a similar way, organizations Beyond Discomfort recognize that the only way DEI will live in the hearts and minds of all staff is if they are given a platform to share their stories. Internal storytelling campaigns help employees understand the impact of exclusion and what they can do. They humanize DEI so that it doesn't feel like a 'woolly, soft' endeavour, but is connected to real people who work in the organization. It is both remarkable and inspiring when colleagues show the courage to share their often hidden and painful lived experiences with others in their organization. And the honour of hearing this raw truth often provokes a commitment to do more. Why? Because storytelling ignites our imagination and enhances empathy. When we hear someone's story, we walk in their shoes and therefore feel their pain. Organizations using this approach often supplement the videos with resources and an invitation to discuss what they can do to be better allies.

For those with a Cheerleading or Proof-Seeking Way of Being, this stark evidence of a different reality and different truth is vital. It encourages all staff to lean in to the discomfort of seeing someone else's pain through perspective-taking and empathy. For those who have a fear of the unknown, it provides concrete evidence of inequity by opening a small window into someone's daily struggle to fit in. It motivates and inspires people who have a fear of complexity to set aside their concern of saying or doing the wrong thing, because the current state of play is far from good enough. Equally as valuable, it signposts to all who work in an organization that it is open to and encouraging of uncomfortable conversations around typically taboo diversity topics.

Depending on the history and demographics of the organization, asking people to engage in these discussions can be completely foreign. In my interview in 2023 with Gareth Hind, Head of Equality, Diversity and Inclusion at First Bus, he described the challenges of creating new conversations in a very traditional transport organization:

> We're 89% male and it has a very generational feel to it – I often have conversations where people tell me that their dad was a driver and grandpa was a driver... so, it is quite an insular industry. As such, there's a lot around, 'We've always done it this way', which is very prevalent because there hasn't been diversity of thought coming into the business, and precisely what we are working on.

However, whilst DEI conversations generate heightened levels of discomfort within organizations that are particularly steeped in patriarchy and tradition, the dialogue can happen if people feel safe. At First Bus, one initiative within their comprehensive DEI strategy was an inclusion programme called Celebrating Our Differences. Each module allowed space for people to notice their beliefs and traditions within the organization and openly share their inner conflict of embracing the DEI work. For example, they discussed the value placed on banter in creating a fun work environment, opening an interactive conversation around intent versus impact. Alongside an increase in their quarterly inclusion index, they are now seeing changes in what people are thinking about. For example, leaders are now reaching out for support when they haven't achieved gender balance in their shortlist of candidates for a post.

Bringing people together through workshops where they can discuss DEI concepts is a great place to start. Firstly, workshops are a significant investment of time and money, which automatically establishes the importance placed on DEI by all who work there (naturally helped if the senior leaders themselves attend). Secondly, this creates a platform for new conversations and stories to be shared, with valuable learning between colleagues about their different experiences. Thirdly, this can be the catalyst for a cultural shift, where the safety and learning created within the workshops extends beyond and starts to permeate all aspects of organizational life. In my interview with Faran Johnson, she described what embedded DEI looks like:

> Dialogue gets created at every point — in a performance management conversation, and in a first telephone conversation with a headhunter. It's how we work with our suppliers. It happens when we're exiting people (voluntary or involuntary). It's present with the partners we're working with, the communities that we're working in, the customer groups that we represent.

Once everyone in the organization starts observing new, uncomfortable conversations taking place, where staff share experiences and feelings and are offered safe spaces to practise through active encouragement, there is an inevitable DEI snowball effect.

Pushing past personal passions

I can't tell you the number of times I have heard a senior male leader say that gender equality is important to them because they have a daughter. This is positive, of course, and being an inclusive leader is filled with moments of sudden recognition of inequities you hadn't seen before. However, it is then tempting for that senior leader to just stay in the 'gender lane'. They passionately advocate and amplify women's voices and are seen to be a role model, but for gender inclusion specifically.

What you should be aiming for is embedding DEI as part of the business conversation so that you and your fellow leaders are role modelling and advocating for equity and inclusion holistically. This is far more stretching and uncomfortable than aligning leadership DEI work to what you are personally passionate about. To aid this, you and other senior colleagues could sponsor a different diversity group.

Of course, you may have very little knowledge of that community. For one client, we ran expert-led webinars on each of their diversity 'pillars' so that senior sponsors felt reassured they had a foundational level of understanding and an opportunity to ask questions. You could read articles or watch TED Talks to help build knowledge and confidence in your sponsorship role.

Going global

The complexity of DEI multiplies with every additional country and region a business operates in. I was delivering a DEI talent programme for a client headquartered in the US but with large presence in Europe and the Middle East and Africa (EMEA) as well as a growing presence in the Asia–Pacific region. In one workshop in 2022, we were discussing which groups of people were dominant (had privilege and power) in their organization. The discussion amongst some of the EMEA participants spoke volumes about their feelings of exclusion:

'Everything is US-centric – all the events take place there, all key strategic decisions are made there, and they listen more to people's views who are based there.'

'Yes, I agree. It can be small things, like all communication about events is always given in Eastern Time, and so we always need to convert to our region.'

'And, actually, meetings are generally at a time that is convenient for the US. I am the only London-based member of my team, all the rest are in the US, and they often dismiss my opinions; I don't feel my views carry much weight. I've been in the team for a year now and I still don't feel part of it.'

It's clear how this proximity bias occurs. As a company expands, it usually replicates everything that made it successful, including its cultural habits, to the new satellite offices. Leaders are keen to preserve the brand and achieve consistency in interaction with the market in every part of the world. As the head office is the largest site, and generally where the executive team is based, all activities and decisions are centred around that. People are more likely to be listened to, noticed and promoted if they are based there, making those in the regional offices feel undermined and their views less valued.

One way to counteract this is by creating a talent mobility scheme, which can provide opportunities for global talent to work in the head office, both for their own development and to increase visibility of their expertise. This is arguably even more vital for successful globalization, as it would allow senior leaders to immediately gain diversity of thought and culture and inject valuable insight into what will and won't work in local offices and markets. There is discomfort, of course, for some leaders in letting go of their belief of what 'being global' means. On my podcast, Claire Brody shared:

> You have a global strategy, and you thought, 'We're going to scale this out across our regions', which already takes away from regions being able to feed into that global strategy. So, I would almost reframe that to say instead of scaling a strategy to make it global, why don't you empower your regions to inform you, as you're creating that global strategy with what makes sense within their regions.

Key to creating global inclusion is understanding the historical and cultural nuances that lead to exclusion in each country where the organization operates. For example, racial inequity in the US focuses on Native, Black, Asian, Hispanic and Latino Americans, but imposing this lens on communities in Asia would be a mistake. In countries such as Singapore, Malaysia, Japan, Taiwan, China and South Korea, racism is more subtle and tends to be related to xenophobia; as well, there can be within-country urban versus rural regional discrimination. In India, colourism is prevalent, as darker-skinned people, women in particular, face abuse and are looked down upon. The best global strategy is, therefore, to empower and create accountability at local level. Each country should have its own definition of DEI and be able to set country-specific goals within the broader company-wide strategy.

In my podcast discussion with Christian Hug, previously Vice President of LifeWorks & Inclusion at Discovery, he discussed their 2020 global training programme, which focused on understanding bias, respect, integrity and allyship:

> We could have rolled this out as one product for our global population, which is around 10,000 people. What we decided, though, is to take a look at how examples are going to translate in the different markets... So we ended up with about 30 nuanced unconscious bias trainings, which were all recorded in local language, rather than buying an off-the-peg product.

Tensions inevitably arise when the broader organizational DEI values don't align with each of the countries the organization operates in. An example of this would be an organization that wants to demonstrate allyship for the LGBTQ+ community but operates in countries where people who identify as LGBTQ+ are criminalized and imprisoned for private, consensual same-sex sexual intimacy. At the time of writing, 65 jurisdictions fall into this category, of which 12 impose the death penalty.[2] Where is the line between striving for an organization that is inclusive of all versus respecting the local culture and legislation? Is the organization able to step in to protect a member of staff who has been arrested in their country for illegal sexual activity? No, even if the organization itself believes this to be unjust. Can the organization show support and solidarity through hosting events, raising awareness and educating staff, and by creating safe and, if need be, anonymous spaces for global LGBTQ+ employees? Yes, absolutely.

Recognizing that safety is constantly in flux depending on the context is vital for a global organization. For example, I have made it a point to include my pronouns in my email signature and on social channels. This is to demonstrate my allyship of the LGBTQ+ community. However, if I was working in a country where being LGBTQ+ was illegal, or if I was working with clients from these countries, I may fear that this act could be misinterpreted as me being gay or queer myself, which could have serious consequences for my relationship with these clients. In our podcast discussion, Bendita Cynthia Malakia illustrated through a personal story: 'People I worked with knew that I identified as bisexual or queer, and we were in countries that require you to report people who you know are queer – there's criminalization for people that don't report. And so, what do you do in these circumstances?'

Good question – there is no clear answer. Global organizations need to recognize this challenging and complex situation for both the LGBTQ+ member of staff, who may not feel safe to travel to satellite offices or client locations in the affected countries, and for any colleagues who are travelling with them. Cultural intelligence is more than just understanding the nuances of different cultures; it's about having the foresight to know where clashes or tensions could play out and being able to actively address them. Bendita took personal responsibility for this situation by asking her colleagues to let her know if they didn't feel comfortable travelling with her. In addition to this, an organization Beyond Discomfort can open safe dialogue for staff to share their views and feelings about these political, ethical and emotional topics. This way, people can acknowledge and unpack the inner struggle associated with wanting to be an ally but having to take personal risk in doing so. It's also important for staff to share their expectations of support from the organization, particularly those who are part of the marginalized community.

⟳ Being future ready

As a leader, the data you need to support your DEI decision-making isn't always accessible – sometimes it's non-existent. In order to consciously bring a different mix of people into conversations and get intersectional perspectives, the organization needs a full range of demographic data, and staff need to trust the organization to protect personal information. Many organizations are running 'self ID' campaigns, explaining why this data is important to inclusion and actively encouraging everyone to disclose their diversity.

When collecting this data, its vital to look ahead and consider what DEI-related societal changes are on the horizon so that the questions you ask are future-proofed. In my podcast discussion with Marc McKenna-Coles, he noted that a previous employer was limited in their inclusion efforts due to systems in other organizations:

> Research shows, in the next decade or so, around 20% of the younger generation will not identify with a binary gender. So, as organizations, we need to account for this. Now, we know that there are some challenges – for example, government systems. But there are always ways around that. For example, if someone identified as non-binary, our system would automatically generate a message to say: 'Due to some third parties, we do require a binary gender, so please contact HR to have a discussion.' We want them to know that we are not disrespecting their gender identity, but unfortunately we are restricted by other organizations that just haven't moved with the times.

Taking a stand

In January 2021, a UK train conductor dialled in to a company webinar on the topic of White privilege. At the end of the webinar, he turned round to his wife, who was also at home, and, not realizing he was unmuted, said: 'Do you know what I really wanted to ask, and I wish I had? Do they have Black privilege in other countries? So, if you're in Ghana…?'[3] He didn't realize other attendees could hear his remarks, and several people made complaints. The train conductor later received a call from his line manager, who suspended him from duty until further investigation. Following a hearing, he was dismissed for gross misconduct due to breach of the company's DEI policy. Was his question racist? Perhaps, but not necessarily. It seems to me that he was more likely coming from a place of ignorant curiosity rather than deliberately minimizing the existence of White supremacy. It's a perfect example of an organization taking a zero-tolerance approach to exclusion and missing the goal by several hundred metres.

The thing is, an inclusive culture isn't created through generating widespread fear of stepping out of line and saying the wrong thing (funny that). These actions are often born out of the organization's fear of internal criticism if it isn't seen to be taking a stand on discrimination. News can quickly snowball out of the organization and before you know it, it is in the media limelight for all of the wrong reasons. An organization Beyond Discomfort acknowledges that everyone who works there still has a lot to learn. If incidences like the one just described do occur, which they generally will as soon as the organization starts opening healthy discussion on DEI topics, it is able to take in the views of the offended party and support the other person or group to understand their perspective, and vice versa. For clarity, this isn't about forcing anyone to change their views – everyone has a right to believe what they wish and organizations should create a safe space for all. There is always the risk of things going horribly wrong and spiralling out of control, but as more people learn what it means to collaborate across difference, the less likely it is that this will happen.

Taking a stand for DEI needs to expand to each touchpoint the organization has, including with suppliers and clients, but this is more complex and riskier. The organization needs to be very clear where they draw the line in working with suppliers or clients that display values counter to DEI. Take the recruitment industry, for example – it's fast-paced and competitive. Sales figures are everything, and that means finding the right candidates to put in front of clients so that they are happy and come back again for future hires. If they aren't happy, then the market is filled with other agencies who will be able to satisfy. I gained insight into the consequences of this when facilitating a workshop in 2020 with sales consultants, one of whom talked about a client who said explicitly that they only wanted to see candidates from a White background. The consultant was concerned about this but didn't know what to do. They said that if they sent a range of diverse candidates, the client would only choose the White candidates to take forward. But if they refused, then the client would just go to another agency and they would lose the work.

He also had a personal financial incentive to place a candidate, since his bonus relied on him achieving or surpassing his sales target, and this outweighed the company's DEI endeavour.

An organization Beyond Discomfort recognizes that its historical supplier or client base may not align to their DEI values and is willing to hold them to account even if it means losing business. Now, this is perhaps easier said than done, as there doesn't appear to be a commercial rationale. However, in expressing to the world what they stand for and taking action to demonstrate it, organizations will attract clients that hold DEI of equal importance. These organizations are growing in number and are actively pursuing an ethical supply chain. Despite the short-term risk and uncertainty, the longer-term gain is a value-aligned organization which can send a powerful message to its employees, enhancing their trust and establishing accountability.

Organizations, and particularly leading brands, have influence in society and, therefore, in many ways have a responsibility to move conversations into the public space. However, this isn't the same as opening the dialogue within their organization – the outside world isn't made up of liberal, open-minded employees. A number of companies have been surprised at the wave of negative comments they received as a result of posting support for marginalized communities. It can be both overwhelming to manage and detrimental to their image and reputation. Whilst it is far easier and safer to delete the post and close the conversation, an organization Beyond Discomfort recognizes that there will always be some form of backlash and continues to show solidarity to these communities anyway. This means overcoming the fear of putting their views into the world in the knowledge that their power and influence can support real change.

Chapter summary

Organizations Beyond Discomfort have the collective courage to delve deeply beneath the surface to analyse their culture, resisting the superficial 'quick wins' just to prove action is being taken. They want to achieve more than diverse representation – they want to know that everyone in their organization feels included and that they belong. Examples such as the BBC's 50:50 Project highlight the benefits of adopting a data-led, transparent, target-based approach to creating change.

Without doubt, a successful DEI strategy needs to be driven from the top, but equally it should be informed by everyone in the organization. Global organizations have the additional complexity of navigating cultural, political and legislative differences, which means flexing strategy to meet local needs. Finally, organizations need to be prepared to make risky, uncomfortable decisions to stand by their DEI values, even if that means challenging stakeholders, clients and suppliers or sharing their views publicly. In essence, it takes the majority of people in the organization to lead Beyond Discomfort, most notably those at the very top, which takes time, effort and continuous reinforcement. It is possible and it is definitely worth it.

Organizational actions of discomfort

An organization Beyond Discomfort can only be achieved through a collective senior leadership endeavour to place DEI at the heart of everything it does. Overcoming barriers due to concern for self, lack of self-awareness, questioning of DEI fairness or believing DEI has already been achieved (as outlined in Chapters 2, 3 and 4) is fundamental and, therefore, must be the starting point. Here are some of my personal recommendations for what organizations should focus on:

o   Practise and role model discomfort by inviting people to share their experiences of what it is like to work in the organization. Where psychological safety hasn't yet been earned, this can be through an anonymized inclusion survey. But, eventually, this can be done through sharing case studies and videos of staff stories.

o   Share insights from your inclusion survey and analysis around gender, ethnicity and other pay gaps, your career progression data and your demographic information for succession planning. This transparency, even if it doesn't show a totally rosy picture, is vital to gaining trust in the organization's integrity and establishing momentum across the whole organization to take action.

o   Ensure your DEI strategy is more than just transactional quick wins that focus only on diversity and representation. Be bold and look at root causes so your actions push for transformational culture change. Tailor your strategy to each local site or country so that everyone feels seen and heard, and people want to get behind the work because it makes sense.

o   Pair a senior leader sponsor with a DEI focus area, related to your DEI strategy, so they can actively engage with the respective employee resource group or other working group. Equip them through webinars, direct them to further resources and upskill them on what it means to be an ally.

o   Put time and ongoing energy into your DEI strategy. Make sure it is clearly linked to your overall organizational strategy and discuss progress, alongside all other strategic priorities, at least once a month.

o   Invest in an inclusive leadership programme where senior leaders have space to self-reflect, ask questions, challenge each other's thinking, broaden their knowledge of DEI and gain a sense of togetherness and shared commitment. Over time, all people managers should be included in these activities.

o   Invite new voices around the decision-making table. This can be in the form of reverse mentoring (see Chapter 3), a shadow board (also discussed in Chapter 3) or a talent mobility programme, or through creating clear communication channels from employee resource groups, a DEI committee and champions (as discussed earlier in this chapter).

o   Run events throughout the year with internal speakers and external guests to share stories and open new conversations. These events can be centred around DEI calendar events such as National Inclusion Week, Black History Month or International Women's Day and International Men's Day, but don't just stick to these times of year to discuss the topics.

o   Continue to measure the inclusion culture at various time points and share the insights to reinforce the change you are seeing and emphasize that you are not becoming complacent about the need for ongoing work. Celebrate successes and acknowledge everyone's contribution in this effort.

Final words

As busy leaders, we have little time to reflect on how our deeply held values and beliefs influence how we interpret the world or why our emotions are activated when something jars with us. When it comes to DEI, we tend to be more aware of how the enhanced focus on diversity in our organization, and in society more generally, sparks a series of thoughts and questions: 'This doesn't make sense.' 'It isn't fair. I can't help my privilege.' 'I don't understand why we're meant to see people's differences.' 'What exactly should I be saying or doing to be more inclusive?' 'What happens if I say or do the wrong thing?' So in the end, the uncertainty, fears and discomfort evoked by DEI can actually limit our learning and action.

Organizations wanting to make progress in DEI naturally want their leaders to take active roles. For example, they might be a sponsor of an employee resource group, support a positive action programme or participate in a panel discussion at an all-staff event. But, if leaders are operating with elements of the Disconcerted, Proof-Seeking or Cheerleading Ways of Being, they will likely show less energy for the work, and culture change will be much slower as a result. I hope I have encouraged organizations to reconsider their starting point — inclusive leadership involves deep psychological work which is hugely uncomfortable but shouldn't be avoided.

I set out the Beyond Discomfort® model in this book to help you reflect on your way of observing the world. Remember that the purpose isn't for you to find your 'fit', but to support a deeper process of self-reflection on how your own life story, belief systems and personal circumstances shape your response to DEI. I believe that we'll only be able to achieve equity and inclusion once most leaders lean into this. I am, of course, realistic about the fact that not everyone will want to or, indeed, have the capacity to do so. That's OK – I didn't write this book to 'convert' you or get you to do something you don't want to do. But if you find you are resisting or questioning your organization's DEI work, then I hope this book has provoked thought and understanding as to why. If all leaders took this initial step, I believe we would find it much easier to enter into healthy and open discussions to unravel the complexity and find a path together.

Summary of key points

I offer here a few thoughts on some of the key takeaways from this book. You may have had numerous other moments of provocation and learning, all of which are valuable and which you should hang on to, reflect on and use to guide your leadership. I am always happy to hear about these, so please reach out and share.

o DEI work and in particular creating equity can cause people with majority characteristics to feel sidelined, guilty for their privilege and unfairly treated. It is important that if you feel this way, you recognize this and reflect on what specifically evokes this.

o Believing in a meritocratic system isn't realistic given the biases we all carry and our human desire to connect to people like us. Whilst it may be deeply uncomfortable, you may want to spend time revisiting your narrative about your earned successes in life and consider how your diversity characteristics may have influenced your experiences.

o Binary thinking is a common human pitfall and causes us to believe that our way of observing the world is true for all. This is both unhelpful and limiting in our leadership of others. It can be tough to hear other people's truths and confusing if you haven't seen any evidence of them. It's important to create space for people to share their truths with you, recognize the emotions that are evoked in you when they do and use this new knowledge to shape your leadership.

o Strength in leadership doesn't come from having all the answers, but from showing awareness that you don't. Reflecting on your definition of leadership and allowing the collective wisdom of other people's realities to inform your perspective and decision-making is key to inclusion.

o DEI holds many paradoxes, one of which is that we need to see people's differences for them to feel included. Discomfort is inevitably present when we open ourselves to seeing people's differences, because we suddenly become aware of invisible inequities that we may have unintentionally contributed to. Actively seeking out inequities and supporting work to dismantle systemic bias is vital to creating change.

o Inclusive leaders don't have to permanently operate Beyond Discomfort – this would be unrealistic. However, they should practise discomfort regularly, noticing when their emotions and fears get the better of them and considering why. This continual process of self-reflection, navigating emotions so that you move into more productive places, and being open to learning by doing (despite the potential mistakes) is what will set you apart as a truly inclusive leader.

o To achieve organizational inclusion, most or all leaders need to be willing to practise discomfort, both individually and collectively, in their decision-making. This takes organizational vulnerability to another level by opening up new, uncomfortable conversations internally, being transparent about where the current issues are and publicly showing allyship. This maturity takes a significant amount of work, investment and time, but the benefits for employee well being and for the bottom line and organizational sustainability are well worth it.

Glossary

Ableist – a person who discriminates against people with mental disorders and physical disabilities.

Accent bias – prejudice towards individuals and communities who speak with an accent that is different from the majority group.

Active allyship – when someone is committed and prepared to take meaningful and consistent action to promote equity and inclusion.

Affinity bias – a tendency to favour people who are like us, those who share similar interests, backgrounds and experiences with us. This leads to unconscious rejection of those who are different from us.

Assessment – evaluation of a situation or person based on what we deem to be relevant information.

Attention deficit hyperactivity disorder (ADHD) – a disorder that typically involves persistent difficulty in maintaining attention and concentration, and display of impulsive and restless behaviour. It often displays differently between genders.

Binary bias – a way to help us simplify information by grouping data, people or things into two categories. This leads to making assumptions and overgeneralizing.

Bystander – a person who is present at an incident of discrimination or abuse but doesn't get involved. In these situations, people take no action because the presence of others makes them feel less responsible.

Diversity – the range of human differences. These can also be demographic differences, to do with race, social class, ethnicity, gender, sexual orientation, physical ability, cognitive processes, religion, nationality, age and so on.

Equality – when every individual and group of people are given the same rights to resources and opportunities, regardless of their circumstances, identities and backgrounds.

Equity – fairness and justice for every individual, which acknowledges that we don't all have the same starting point and that some people have advantages and some don't.

Exclusionary behaviour – attitudes, comments or actions that isolate and alienate others. These are often insensitive and inappropriate words or actions, which can lead to the person feeling unsafe and unwelcomed, or even more damaging outcomes.

Experiential learning – the process of learning by doing and then reflecting on this experience to develop personal understanding, knowledge and skills.

Gaslighting – a form of psychological abuse. It is a manipulative tactic that a person uses to gain power or control another individual by provoking self-doubt and uncertainty, which can be harmful to their mental health.

Growth mindset – the belief that skills can be developed over time and that people can take active steps to do so.

Intersectionality – the overlap and the interaction of an individual's various marginalized identities, which can lead to cumulative discrimination where those identities are marginalized.

Microaggression – an act, remark or assumption that subtly, indirectly or unintentionally expresses discrimination against an individual or a marginalized group.

Neurodivergent – when an individual's neurological functions behave differently from what is classified as typical or normal. Within this category, there is ADHD, autism, dyspraxia, dyslexia and more.

Neurodiversity – the natural diversity of human brains, which acknowledges that everyone thinks differently.

Neurotypical – individuals whose brain functions, behaviours and processing are considered usual or expected by society.

Performative allyship – an act of publicly appearing committed to a cause but without taking any significant action. It is typically motivated by the desire for personal benefit and not with an intention to influence real change.

Positive action – a range of measures introduced to counter the impact of structural discrimination. It generally offers support and development to marginalized groups to help them overcome the disadvantages they face.

Privilege – a right or benefit given to some but not others. Typically, this person gains more advantage over another because of their social position, background, wealth and so on.

Psychological safety – when people feel they can express their ideas and share aspects of their identity without fear of negative consequences or judgement.

Saviourism – a behaviour or policy that frames a group of people as needing to be saved. 'White saviourism' refers to a situation where a White person is perceived as rescuing, liberating or uplifting people from marginalized communities.

Unconscious bias – a positive or negative attitude towards a person or group. This is played out when we act on deeply ingrained stereotypes and attitudes formed from our experiences, upbringing and environment.

Upstander – a person who actively speaks up, supports and defends an individual, a cause or a belief.

Woke – someone who is well informed about social and racial injustice and inequality.

Workplace inclusion – embracing people's differences and integrating everyone in the workplace regardless of their identities. This ensures that people feel valued and have a sense of belonging, which then creates a workplace where people feel comfortable and confident to be themselves.

Xenophobia – the attitudes, prejudice and behaviour that excludes people who are perceived as foreigners from the community, society or national identity.

Gender and sexuality terms

It's worth noting that DEI language, and specifically gender and sexuality terms, are ever evolving. The following list covers some of the key terms in use today. I haven't referred to all of these terms in the book; however,

I regularly come across leaders who find the language around gender and sexuality both confusing and overwhelming, so I have included the list in the hope that it helps if you find yourself in this position. This isn't an exhaustive list and the definitions aren't strict, but I hope that it helps you understand language that may be less familiar to you.

Ace – a broad term used to describe someone who has little or no experiences of sexual attraction.

Allo – people who feel sexual and romantic attraction towards others.

Aro – an umbrella term that describes a lack of or occasional experiences of romantic attraction.

Aromantic – a person who does not experience romantic attraction. Some experience sexual attraction, whilst others don't.

Asexual – an individual who does not identify as having a sexual desire towards other individuals. Some experience romantic attraction, whilst others do not.

Bisexual – a person who is sexually and/or romantically attracted to more than one gender or sex.

Cisgender – someone whose gender identity is the same as the sex they were assigned at birth.

Demiromantic – an umbrella term that describes those who may only feel romantically attracted to people with whom they have formed a strong emotional bond.

Demisexual – an umbrella term that describes those who may only feel sexually attracted to people with whom they have formed a strong emotional bond.

Gay (or homosexual) – a generic term that refers to those who are solely attracted to the same sex. It is typically used to refer to a man who has romantic and/or sexual attraction towards men. Non-binary people can also identify as gay.

Gender dysphoria – when a person is uncomfortable or distressed because there is misalignment between their sex assigned at birth and their gender identity.

Gender identity – the gender that an individual identifies as, whether male, female, non-binary or any other gender, which may or may not correspond to their sex assigned at birth.

Gender reassignment – a way to describe a person's gender transition. This can involve having medical involvement, changing one's name and pronouns, dressing differently or living as the self-identified gender.

Gender transitioning – the process that trans people undertake to live as the gender with which they identify.

Grey – an umbrella term which defines those who experience attraction sometimes, rarely or under certain conditions.

Heterosexual – a person who is romantically and/or sexually attracted to the opposite gender.

Intersex – when someone is born with a number of variants of physiological or physical traits that are outside the binary definition of gender.

Lesbian – a woman who has romantic and/or sexual attraction exclusively towards women.

LGBTQ+ – an acronym for lesbian, gay, bisexual, trans, queer or questioning, with the plus sign referring to non-heterosexuals who don't feel they are represented by these terms.

Non-binary – an umbrella term that refers to people who don't identify as a man or a woman.

Pansexual – an individual who has a sexual or romantic orientation towards all genders and sexual orientations.

Queer – an umbrella term to describe sexual and gender identities other than straight or cisgender.

Questioning – those who are exploring their gender identity, sexual orientation or both.

Trans – an umbrella term to describe a person whose gender identity is not the same as their assigned sex at birth.

Transgender man – someone who was assigned female at birth but lives and identifies as a man.

Transgender woman – someone who was assigned male at birth but lives and identifies as a woman.

Two-spirited – often attributed to Indigenous American people who identify as having multiple energies and spirits within them.

Notes

Introduction

1 A. Sieler, *Coaching to the Human Soul: Ontological Coaching and Deep Change*, Volume 1 (Newfield Australia, 2003).
2 *Emma Watson Facebook Q&A about HeForShe – International Women's Day 2015*, YouTube (8 March 2015). Available from: www.youtube.com/watch?v=n4xzvDzP-lA
3 E. Kübler-Ross, *On Death and Dying* (Touchstone, 1969).
4 D. Kahneman, *Thinking Fast and Slow* (Macmillan, 2011).
5 S.K. Sandberg, *Lean In: Women, Work and the Will to Lead* (WH Allen, 2015).

Chapter 1

1 'Beyond Vietnam, a time to break silence', address at Riverside Church, New York (4 April 1967).
2 K. Crenshaw, 'Demarginalizing the intersection of race and sex: A Black feminist critique of antidiscrimination doctrine, feminist theory and antiracist politics', *University of Chicago Legal Forum*, 1989 (1), Article 8 (1989). Available at: https://chicagounbound.uchicago.edu/uclf/vol1989/iss1/8
3 McKinsey & Company, *Diversity Wins: How Inclusion Matters* (McKinsey & Company, 2020). Available from: www.mckinsey.com/~/media/mckinsey/featured%20insights/diversity%20and%20inclusion/diversity%20wins%20how%20inclusion%20matters/diversity-wins-how-inclusion-matters-vf.pdf
4 Credit Suisse Research Institute, *The CS Gender 3000 in 2021: Broadening the Diversity Discussion* (Credit Suisse Research Institute, 2021). Available from: www.credit-suisse.com/media/assets/corporate/docs/about-us/research/publications/csri-2021-gender-3000.pdf

5 K.W. Phillips, 'How diversity makes us smarter', *Scientific American* (1 October 2014). Available from: www.scientificamerican.com/article/how-diversity-makes-us-smarter/

6 Accenture, *Getting to Equal 2019: Creating a Culture that Drives Innovation* (Accenture, 2019). Available from: www.accenture.com/content/dam/accenture/final/a-com-migration/thought-leadership-assets/accenture-equality-equals-innovation-gender-equality-research-report-iwd-2019.pdf

7 Quotes from podcast discussions have been lightly edited for clarity and context whilst attempting to be true to the original work. All podcast episodes were recorded during 2020–23, and they can be found at www.avenirconsultingservices.com/podcast

8 J. Cook, '"Racist" passport photo system rejects image of a young black man despite meeting government standards', *The Telegraph* (19 September 2019).

9 Snap Inc., *Diversity Annual Report 2020* (Snap Inc., 2020). Available from: https://diversity.snap.com/resources

10 K. Rice, I. Prichard, M. Tiggemann and A. Slater, 'Exposure to Barbie: Effects on thin-ideal internalisation, body esteem, and body dissatisfaction among young girls', *Body Image*, 19, 142–49 (2016).

11 *Gross sales of Mattel's Barbie brand worldwide from 2012 to 2022*, Statista. Available from: www.statista.com/statistics/370361/gross-sales-of-mattel-s-barbie-brand/

12 H.J. Parkinson, '#AirBnBWhileBlack hashtag highlights potential race bias on app', *The Guardian* (5 May 2016). Available from: www.theguardian.com/technology/2016/may/05/airbnbwhileblack-hashtag-highlights-potential-racial-bias-rental-app

13 M. Murgia and D. Lee, 'Airbnb pricing algorithm led to increased racial disparities, study finds', *Financial Times* (13 May 2021).

14 *Airbnb diversity data H1 2022*, Airbnb. Available from: https://news.airbnb.com/airbnb-diversity-data-h1-2022/

15 *Rankings Gobal RepTrak® 100*, RepTrak. Available from: https://reptrak.com/rankings/

16 LinkedIn Talent Solutions, *The Future of Recruiting 2023* (LinkedIn Talent Solutions, 2023). Available from: https://business.linkedin.com/talent-solutions/resources/future-of-recruiting

17 D. Hines, 'Alan Sugar slams people who work from home as a "bunch of lazy layabouts"', *The Standard* (14 December 2022). Available from: www.standard.co.uk/showbiz/alan-sugar-work-from-home-lazy-layabouts-b1047169.html

18 A. Cuthbertson and G. Kilander, 'Elon Musk doubles down on threat to fire Tesla workers who refuse to come back to the office', *Independent* (2 June 2022). Available from: www.independent.co.uk/tech/elon-musk-tesla-remote-working-b2091813.html

19 *Families and the labour market, UK: 2021*, Office for National Statistics. Available from: www.ons.gov.uk/employmentandlabourmarket/peopleinwork/employmentandemployeetypes/articles/familiesandthelabourmarketengland/2021

20 *Employment characteristics of families*, US Bureau of Labor Statistics. Available from: www.bls.gov/news.release/pdf/famee.pdf

21 B. Franklin and T. Singh, *Fair Growth: Opportunities for Economic Renewal* (Centre for Progressive Policy, 2023). Available from: www.progressive-policy.net/publications/fair-growth

22 J. Dixon, F. Ruby and E. Clery, *Single Parents in 2023* (Gingerbread). Available from: www.gingerbread.org.uk/wp-content/uploads/2023/03/Single-Parents-in-2023-Single-Parents-Day-report.pdf

23 *Families and the labour market, UK; 2021*, Office for National Statistics.

24 S. Kramer, *U.S. has world's highest rate of children living in single-parent households*, Pew Research Center (12 December 2019). Available from: www.pewresearch.org/short-reads/2019/12/12/u-s-children-more-likely-than-children-in-other-countries-to-live-with-just-one-parent/

25 L. Radcliffe, C. Cassell and F. Malik, 'Providing, performing and protecting: The importance of work identities in negotiating conflicting work–family ideals as a single mother', *British Journal of Management*, 33, 890–905 (2022). Available from: https://onlinelibrary.wiley.com/doi/pdf/10.1111/1467-8551.12472

26 *Is hybrid working here to stay?* Office for National Statistics (23 May 2022). Available from: www.ons.gov.uk/employmentandlabourmarket/peopleinwork/employmentandemployeetypes/articles/ishybridworkingheretostay/2022-05-23

27 Working Families, *Working Families Index 2022: Families and Flexible Working Post Covid-19* (Working Families, 2020). Available from: workingfamilies.org.uk/wp-content/uploads/2022/05/Working-Families-Index-2022-Highlights-Report.pdf

28 DaddiLife, *The Millennial Dad at Work* (DaddiLife, 2019). Available from: www.daddilife.com/wp-content/uploads/2019/05/The-Millenial-Dad-at-Work-Report-2019.pdf

29 *Working Dads Employer Awards*, Music, Football, Fatherhood (1 March 2022). Available from: https://musicfootballfatherhood.com/2022/03/01/working-dads-employer-awards-recognising-inclusive-employers-for-dads/

30 *Gen Z and the end of work as we know it*, World Economic Forum Annual Meeting (19 May 2022). Available from: www.weforum.org/agenda/2022/05/gen-z-don-t-want-to-work-for-you-here-s-how-to-change-their-mind/

31 *Welcome to Generation Z*, Deloitte. Available from: www2.deloitte.com/us/en/pages/consumer-business/articles/understanding-generation-z-in-the-workplace.html

32 Workforce Institute @ Kronos, *Full Report: Generation Z in the Workplace* (Kronos Incorporated, 2019). Available from: https://workforceinstitute.org/wp-content/uploads/2019/11/Full-Report-Generation-Z-in-the-Workplace.pdf

33 In 2004, they created Blockbuster Online, but it was already years behind Netflix and they had lost out on valuable market share.

34 GWI, *Generation Alpha: The Real Picture* (GWI, 2022).

35 World Economic Forum, *Future of Jobs Report 2023: Insight Report May 2023* (World Economic Forum, 2023). Available from: www3.weforum.org/docs/ WEF_Future_of_Jobs_2023.pdf

Chapter 2

1 *Can we learn to disagree better? An episode from our archive,* The Economist Asks [podcast] (29 December 2022).
Available from: www.economist.com/podcasts/2022/12/29/ can-we-learn-to-disagree-better-an-episode-from-our-archive
2 David Kantor and Sarah Hill, 'Working with an invisible reality', *Training Journal* (August 2014). Available from: www.dialogix.co.uk/wp-content/ uploads/2014/10/TJ-AUGUST-2014-low.17-20.pdf
3 *Michael Holding's moving speech about racism before England's test with West Indies,* Sky (11 September 2020). Available at: https://news.sky.com/video/history-is-written-by-the-people-who-do-the-harm-cricket-commentators-view-of-white-privilege-12024274
4 M. Bertrand and S. Mullainathan, *Are Emily and Greg More Employable than Lakisha and Jamal? A Field Experiment on Labor Market Discrimination* (National Bureaux of Economic Research, 2003). Available from: www.nber.org/system/ files/working_papers/w9873/w9873.pdf
5 P. Grange, *Fear Less: How to Win at Life Without Losing Yourself* (Vermilion, 2020).
6 E. Berne, *The Games People Play: The Basic Handbook of Transactional Analysis* (Ballantine Books, 1996).

Chapter 3

1 P. Grange, *Fear Less: How to Win at Life Without Losing Yourself* (Vermilion, 2020).
2 *Myers-Briggs® overview,* Myers & Briggs Foundation. Available from: www. myersbriggs.org/my-mbti-personality-type/myers-briggs-overview/
3 D. Rosenfeld, *The AIDS epidemic's lasting impact on gay men,* The British Academy (19 February 2018). Available at: www.thebritishacademy.ac.uk/blog/ aids-epidemic-lasting-impact-gay-men/
4 M. Fombo, *No. You cannot touch my hair!* TEDx (2017). Available from: www.ted. com/talks/mena_fombo_no_you_cannot_touch_my_hair_jun_2023

Chapter 4

1 D. Chugh, *The Person You Mean to Be: How Good People Fight Bias* (Harper Business, 2018).
2 R.M. Vijaya and N. Bhullar, 'Colorism and employment bias in India: An experimental study in stratification economics', *Review of Evolutionary Political Economy*, 3 (3), 599–628 (2022).
3 K.J. Norwood (Ed.), *Color Matters: Skin Tone Bias and the Myth of a Postracial America* (Routledge, 2014).
4 Avenir, *Putting Privilege in Its Place: Overcoming Barriers to Workplace Inclusion* (Avenir and University of Liverpool).
Available from: www.avenirconsultingservices.com/reports/
putting-privilege-in-its-place-overcoming-barriers-to-workplace-inclusion
5 See the SEO website at: www.seo-usa.org/
6 M. Obama, *Belonging* (Crown, 2018).
7 J. Kelland, *Caregiving Fathers in the Workplace: Organisational Experiences and the Fatherhood Forfeit* (Palgrave Macmillan, 2022).
8 A. Lee Duckworth, *Grit: The power of passion and perseverance*, TED (April 2013). Available from: www.ted.com/talks/
angela_lee_duckworth_grit_the_power_of_passion_and_perseverance
9 C. Dweck, *The power of believing that you can improve*, TED (November 2014). Available from: www.ted.com/talks/
carol_dweck_the_power_of_believing_that_you_can_improve
10 Avenir, *Unlocking Inclusive Leadership: Creating Manageable Discomfort and Accountability* (Avenir, 2023). Available from: www.avenirconsultingservices.com/reports/unlocking-inclusive-leadership-creating-manageable-discomfort-and-accountability

Chapter 5

1 J. Brown, *How to Be an Inclusive Leader: Your Role in Creating Cultures of Belonging Where Everyone Can Thrive*, 2nd edition (Berrett-Koehler Publishers, 2022).
2 Cited in S. Cain, 'Lizzo removes "harmful" ableist slur from new song Grrrls after criticism', *The Guardian* (14 June 2022).
Available from: www.theguardian.com/music/2022/jun/14/
lizzo-removes-harmful-ableist-slur-from-new-song-grrrls-after-criticism
3 L.J. Ross, *Don't call people out – call them in*, TED (August 2021). Available from: www.ted.com/talks/loretta_j_ross_don_t_call_people_out_call_them_in
4 B. Brown, *Dare to Lead hub*. Available from: https://brenebrown.com/hubs/
dare-to-lead

5 Cited in T. McClure, 'Jacinda Ardern resigns as prime minister of New Zealand', *The Guardian* (19 January 2023). Available from: www.theguardian.com/world/2023/jan/19/jacinda-ardern-resigns-as-prime-minister-of-new-zealand

6 Cited in S. Barr, 'Andy Murray's 10 best feminist moments', *Independent* (9 July 2019). Available from: www.independent.co.uk/life-style/women/andy-murray-wimbledon-2019-feminist-moments-equal-pay-sexism-women-serena-williams-a8996971.html#

7 A.C. Edmundson, *The Fearless Organization: Creating Psychological Safety in the Workplace for Learning, Innovation, and Growth* (Wiley, 2018).

8 See the Happy Place website at: www.happyplaceofficial.co.uk; see Dr Chatterjee's website at: https://drchatterjee.com/

9 See Jon Kabat-Zinn's website at: https://jonkabat-zinn.com/

10 S.C. Hayes, K.D. Strosahl and K.G. Wilson, *Acceptance and Commitment Therapy: The Process and Practice of Mindful Change* (Guilford Press, 2016).

Chapter 6

1 B. Brown [@BreneBrown], *Change is uncomfortable* [Tweet] (27 March 2021).

2 *The issue*, Human Dignity Trust. Available at: www.humandignitytrust.org/

3 A. Webber, 'Train conductor unfairly dismissed after "black privilege" comment', *Personnel Today* (10 August 2020). Available at: www.personneltoday.com/hr/train-conductor-black-privilege-tribunal-west-midlands-trains/

Acknowledgements

Without doubt, this book wouldn't be in this world now if it wasn't for my husband, Matthew. People often ask how I manage a thriving business, two young children and writing a book. The answer is simple: I have an incredible support system and people who believe in me. I am so grateful to you, Matthew, for generously walking the path of vulnerability with me in offering the personal stories I have shared in this book.

I have had so many people cheering me on whilst walking this book-writing path and I am grateful to everyone in my Street Team for this. In particular, thank you to my dear friends and professional colleagues, Dr Hayley Lewis and Clare Harris, who read a number of the draft chapters and provided initial, and much-needed, positive reinforcement that this book was worth writing. To Bonnie St. John, my mentor and friend across the water, thank you for your generosity in offering your wisdom to guide my career and for amplifying my voice through yours.

Thank you to the Avenir team, who are so committed to our mission to create a more equitable and inclusive world and who continuously stretch and facilitate my thinking. In particular, thank you to Carole Searle for running a smooth ship and to Glory Olubori for all your support in ensuring the world knows about the work we do and what we stand for. Thank you also to Joanna Gregory-Chialton for collating research, conducting interviews and working with me to think through the book concept. Also, huge thanks to Dounia Rguyeg for supporting the development of the Beyond Discomfort online tools. When I first started *Why Care?* several years ago, I was incredibly fortunate to come across a best-in-class podcast producer, Mauro Serra of Kenji Productions. Thank you so much, Mauro, for your dedication, high standards and hard work.

Particular thanks to my incredible graphic designer, Tanya Tashkinova, who made my roughly sketched Beyond Discomfort diagram into something worthy of being published. Thanks also to the highly talented Victoria Trum for the beautiful cartoon illustrations.

Thank you to all at Practical Inspiration Publishing and, in particular, Alison Jones for your coaching, which shaped the book, and for holding my hand through this extraordinary authorship process. When all signs directed me to you, I knew there must be a reason. Thank you also to Amy Cuthbertson and Nim Moorthy for your hard work getting the book known to the world and extending the readership far and wide. Also, thanks to my two editors, Liliane Nénot and Maggie Reid, for their meticulous work.

And finally, thank you to my parents for the immeasurable ways you have supported me and all my ambitious endeavours throughout my life. You taught me that my voice matters, that I can grow and be more and that anything is possible. Thank you for your unwavering belief.

Special thanks

A huge thank you to everyone who has contributed to the content of this book – it has made a huge difference having your unique perspectives and stories: Errol Amerasekera, Kristen Anderson, Emmeline Barnes, Sámi Ben-Ali, Sean Betts, Rukasana Bhaijee, Claire Brody, Christina Brooks, Jennifer Brown, Charlotte Cox, Sheri Crosby Wheeler, Bendita Cynthia Malakia, Andrew Fairbairn, Shawna Ferguson, Duncan Forbes, Veronica Frincu, Paolo Gaudiano, Nina Goswami, Dr Pippa Grange, Gareth Hind, Caroline Hollins, Alex Howard, Christian Hug, Faran Johnson, Dr Jasmine Kelland, Veronika Koller, Han-Son Lee, Marc McKenna-Coles, Elvin Nagamootoo, Caroline Nankinga, Marta Pajón Fustes, Pat Phelan, Eric Pliner, Nadya Powell, Yash Puri, Dr Laura Radcliffe, Sophie Smallwood, Bonnie St. John and Devi Virdi.

Thank you to my fabulous Street Team, who I have relied upon throughout my writing process to bounce ideas off, steer my thoughts and read sections of the book: Shazma Ahmed, Rose Cartolari, Darin de Klerk, Jessica de Looy-Hyde, Nilufer Demirkol, Janis Dyer, Joanna Gregory-Chialton, Christiane Gross, Yeşim Guner, Clare Harris, Asad Iqbal, Mya Kirkwood, Ken Kittoe, Dr Hayley Lewis, Andy Lison, Glory Olubori, Jayen Parmar, Jiten Patel, Jonathan Rice, Carole Searle and Aboodi Shabi.

I'm incredibly grateful to my beta readers, who offered their summer reading time, feedback and valuable professional lens: Simon Carter, Claire Gallery-Strong, Kadisha Lewis-Roberts, Rebecca Maitland, Devi Virdi and Dr Simon Walne.

About the author

NADIA NAGAMOOTOO (she/her) is the Founder and CEO of Avenir, a chartered psychologist, MBA and accredited coach with 20 years of experience in the field of systemic culture change, leadership development and organizational strategy. She has worked globally to provoke powerful diversity, equity and inclusion (DEI) conversations at all organizational levels and to develop sustainable inclusive leadership practices.

Her work is fuelled by inner values of fairness, equity and human connection, with a deep desire to see more of these in our world. She is best known for her ability to offer clarity and direction around DEI for her clients and to design innovative, experiential learning approaches, as well as her warm and engaging style.

A prolific and highly sought-after keynote speaker, she has shared her expertise in inclusive leadership, privilege, bias and equity to audiences around the world. She is host of the popular podcast *Why Care?*, where she delves deeply into the complex and uncomfortable world of DEI.

Nadia continues to be publicly recognized for her passion, drive and thought leadership, and she was listed as HR Most Influential Thinker 2023 and was named HR Champion of the Year at the European Diversity Awards 2023.

About Avenir

Avenir guides organizations on their leadership and cultural path towards diversity, equity and inclusion (DEI), with a belief that DEI needs to be driven from the top and embodied by everyone who works there. It is on a mission to broaden awareness, understanding and empathy of people's unique lived experiences whilst providing organizations with a strong foundation for how to create a culture of inclusion for all.

As a psychologist-owned consulting firm with a global team of leading DEI consultants, facilitators and coaches, Avenir designs tailor-made DEI programmes that meet clients where they are, both culturally and in their leadership. This takes deep listening, engagement with the top team and offering a DEI approach that meets the business' needs.

In addition to all-staff engagement and workshops, Avenir offers its clients support in two main areas: creating a data-led DEI strategy using its proprietary online inclusion survey; and a six-month experiential inclusive leadership programme.

Avenir enjoys long-standing relationships with its clients, which signals not only the deep systemic work that is required for cultural change but also the close, trusting partnerships it develops through the team's expertise and, ultimately, the impactful results.

Index

Printed in the USA
CPSIA information can be obtained
at www.ICGtesting.com
JSHW071927160224
57527JS00008B/145